"I have found a new Stream of Life where I may bathe my wearied soul in the coolness of sublimity."

—Corey Ford (1902-1969)
June 9, 1920

Trout Tales

and

Other Angling Stories

Corey Ford Archives, courtesy of the Dartmouth College Library

This book is not dedicated to the memory of Corey Ford, for he lives here in these pages. I should like to think, were he to write this Dedication, that he would think of you—the men and women who cast flies onto cool, sublime streams and understand that fishing is more than sport.

For it *is* more than that...far more.

—Laurie Morrow
Freedom, New Hampshire
January 17, 1995

Trout Tales

and Other Angling Stories

by Corey Ford

Compiled and Edited by Laurie Morrow

Illustrated by Christopher Smith

Table of Contents

Foreword

This book is a compilation of some of the fishing stories of outdoor writer and humorist Corey Ford, who wanted you to think that he was a native New Englander, lifelong outdoorsman, expert shot, and married man.

He was none of these things.

If you've read his "Lower Forty" stories, you'd swear Corey was indeed a native New Englander who shouldered a double gun and cast a line from the time he was a lad in knee-britches. Fact is, Corey was thirty-years old before he learned to shoot and hunt, and almost that old when he took up fly fishing.

Yet he desired to be all these things. As a young man, he moved from his native New York City to New Hampshire (adopting that state as his home of forty years) and established himself as a country squire of sorts. Wildly successful as a writer for magazines such as *The New Yorker*, *Vanity Fair*, and *The Saturday Evening Post*, and of Hollywood screenplays such as *The Canterville Ghost*, Corey was a self-made man who could afford a gentleman's life—though it is evident by the sheer bulk of his literary achievement—five hundred short stories and thirty books—that he worked like heck to achieve financial comfort. He may not have been a crack shot, but that's okay—few are. The thing was, he had an enormous and deep-seated love of the out-of-doors. Corey was happiest when engaged in reeling in anything from a two-pound brook trout to a fifty-pound muskie, and equally delighted missing a close-up partridge on account of a stone wall getting in the way, giving him an excuse—and material for another shooting story. That he was a lifelong bachelor was an unfortunate luck of the draw, and I rather believe Corey wanted a woman even more than the trophy-size rainbow you'll read about in "Rainbows in the Chilean Sky." Alas, he never caught any of them.

James "Corey" Hitchcock Ford, Jr. was born in 1902 in Manhattan, the adored only child of Adelaide and James Ford. Raised in suburban Mount Vernon, his was a happy, middle-class childhood that led to an equally happy youth at Columbia University, where he became editor of the campus humor magazine, *The Jester*. His barbed parodies caught the attention of *Life* magazine, and he snatched a proffered job as a staff writer just months before graduation, forfeiting his degree. He never looked back.

Corey managed to juggle his skyrocketing, high-powered career between both coasts until 1935, when powerful producers such as David O. Selznick of *Gone With the Wind* fame, totally frustrated, ran out of ways to coerce Corey out of some Alaskan trout stream or Deep South quail field to get back to work. This did not affect Corey's reputation or proclivity—he was, after all, a hot property just like contemporary and pal F. Scott Fitzgerald. But that was the year Corey began writing the stuff for which he would become most popular—his outdoor stories.

The first was a fishing humor piece for *Field & Stream*, the direct result of a fan letter to its legendary editor-in-chief, Ray P. Holland, suggesting he nab Corey to write for them. Holland allowed how that was a good idea, and *Field & Stream* became Corey's outdoor-literary home until his death in 1969 at the age of sixty-seven. Of course, Corey wrote for other magazines such as *Outdoor Life*, *Sports Afield*, and the now defunct *Colliers*. The rollicking misadventures of the Lower Forty Shooting, Angling and Inside Straight Club were founded in 1953 on the pages of *Field & Stream* and inspired by this place, my home and Corey's—the still sleepy village of Freedom, New Hampshire.

Each morning, as Corey did, I wake up and look out over "our" rolling, pine-edged field he made famous as the Lower Forty. "Hardscrabble" is a real place, and yes, the people who sparked Corey into creating the characters—Uncle Perk, Angus MacNab, Dexter Sneed, Deacon Godfrey—were real, too. "Doc Hall" was named after Dr. James W. Hall, a friend late in Corey's life and now a writer himself. However, "Judge Parker," the only character not cut from whole cloth, was Corey's great and good friend—the late Judge Parker Merrow, who remains a legend hereabouts.

At the delicate age of forty-nine, Corey moved to Judge Parker's alma mater, Dartmouth, in Hanover, New Hampshire, where he served as the college's writer-in-residence and surrogate father to a number of students. His imposing brick house on the outskirts of the campus became a home away from home for many an undergrad, and some of these now middle-aged men still occasionally knock on the door of the present owners and confide, "Sorry to disturb you. I just wanted to see the old place again. You know, I was happiest here, in this house. Corey was *the best* thing about my college years."

Corey was *the best* about a lot of things. He was charming and witty and a steadfast friend. He became an expert fly fisherman, a fair but serious shot, and the best partner to hunt or fish with, living up to the definition of sportsmanship that Teddy Roosevelt gave to his three sons: "Stand the gaff, play fair; be a good man to camp out with." Corey also was a highly knowledgeable field dog man, devoted to his bloodline of Cloverley English setters, of which Cider was his first. You've read "Just a Dog," perhaps—the open letter Corey wrote to an out-of-state hunter who shot too quickly and injured his bitch, Trout—and then finished the job with a second shot to "put her out of her misery." If so, you know how deep his love of dogs went, and you cried, I'll bet, like the rest of the country.

Corey loved October—to him it was the best time of the year, and so it is. He named his last dog October and set the best outdoor story ever written, "The Road to Tinkhamtown," in autumn's pinnacle. Corey never missed opening day of bird season except during the War. He was nuts about American history and loved his country so well that he enlisted, at age forty, to become an Army Air Corps' chronicler—risking his life many times over to stay alongside the boys, write their story—and, too often, a letter home to a soldier's folks to tell them what a fine son they used to have....

I hope I've given you a sense of the man. If you've never read Corey Ford, you're about to enjoy a smattering from his extensive works—the kind of stories that earned him the reputation of being among the best outdoor writers of his day, or for that matter, any day. Keep this in mind as you turn these pages: Corey loved the idea of being in love—with crisp country air and babbling brooks and grouse cover and blazing sunsets—and yes, with life and living. You'll get a sense of this throughout this book. About halfway through, you'll see he loved women very much—a number of them, actually—but when he died he was alone, without that one gal he could share his life with, and for whom he spent a lifetime searching. Corey died, in fact, without family, leaving just about his entire estate to Dartmouth College.

Which is where I come in.

Corey was not only a prolific writer, but something of a miser as well—not in the sense of being a tightwad; he was the most generous of men—but because he saved every scrap of paper that had anything to do with anything. The literary archives he left Dartmouth College contain everything from receipts for a tank of gas for his Jeep to never-before-published paintings by both his pal at *The Saturday Evening Post*, Norman Rockwell, and a good friend of his who made a fortune with a mouse named Mickey.

And there are his typescripts and manuscripts. Their range portrays the diversity of this complex man—the humorist who made the country's ribs hurt from laughing, the columnist who wrote parodies with a barbed pen, the historian, the romantic, the teacher, and of course, the country gentleman with an obsessive love of the out-of-doors.

In the process of tunneling through the paper trail of Corey Ford's life, I came to fall head-over-heels in love with this guy—a quarter-century too late. And I never met him. So instead, I'm Corey's official biographer and I figure I know him pretty intimately, maybe more than anyone before or after he departed. On the day of the twenty-fifth anniversary of his death, it was good that I found his final resting place, which had been forgotten (he had no funeral); good that I lay flowers on that peaceful spot; and good that the flowers were from his field—our field—the Lower Forty.

Rotten way to start a love affair—but then, I'm afraid that you're about to embark on one, too. For if you've never read Corey Ford, you're going to love his stuff. If ever river water slapped by the tail of a fighting trout has splashed your cheek...if the sun's scorched the back of your neck while you waited in vain for a take on that dry fly you spent hours tying...if you didn't sleep much the night before opening day like an excited child awaiting Santa—in Corey Ford you will find a soulmate.

Laurie Morrow
The Lower Forty
Freedom, New Hampshire
April 9, 1995

Introduction
Corey Ford

*W*hy do people fish? Nary a word is to be found amid all the
encyclopedias and books in the world to explain what perverse
impulse, what freakish strain, what incomprehensible urge causes an otherwise normal and sane citizen to don a pair of uncomfortable rubber
waders, lace a dozen pounds of hobnailed boots onto his aching feet,
truss himself helplessly in canvas vest and landing net and creel, and hike
upstream ten miles in a pouring rain, fighting midges and black flies,
scratching his face on brambles, wincing whenever the elastic strap of his
landing net catches on a twig and lets go like a slingshot, smacking him
smartly between the shoulder blades. Why does he undergo all this in
order to stand patiently all day in icy water up to his hubs, casting his rod
back and forth till his arm aches, wet and sore and blistered and
mosquito-bitten and hungry. And, in all probability, fishless.

Why, indeed?

Is it because he wants the fish to eat? I doubt it. For ten cents, and
one-tenth the amount of time and trouble, he could walk down to the
market and buy a pound of halibut. Moreover, I've seen too many fishermen work an hour to bring a trout to the net, reach down and grab him
firmly behind the gills, release the fly, and then turn him loose again to
disappear under a rock with a final grateful wag of his square tail.

Is it for the sport of casting, then?

Maybe a little. There is no thrill like that of presenting a fly accurately, watching it ride well-cocked down a riffle, and suddenly seeing the
water explode around it in a shower of iridescent drops, feeling the heavy
weight on the line, hearing the skirl of the reel as the captive trout races
for whitewater. I still remember the expression of profound pleasure on
the face of Ted Townsend, who initiated me into the mysteries of dry fly
fishing a quarter of a century ago on the Beaverkill. Ted had paused on

the bank and tied an exquisite copy of the fly that was on the water, a Female Beaverkill, and had cast it across the pool, setting it down as lightly as thistledown on the water. As we watched, a live male fly, with love light shining in his eyes, spotted the artificial female and settled down amorously beside her. A trout rose just then—instead of choosing the real fly, it grabbed Ted's. You can't ask for a nicer tribute to an angler than that.

But I think there is another and deeper reason why people fish. It is an age-old desire that moves all of us—whether dry fly purist, spinner fisherman, saltwater angler, or kid with the willow pole and catawba worm. It is something that cannot be defined, even in an encyclopedia, but the urge is there whenever an angler wades into a new pool, or looks down from a bridge at the water below, or starts in his canoe across a silent lake at dusk. It has something to do with peace, contentment, and soul-satisfaction, and the realization that for a moment at least, nothing else in the world really matters.

– One –

Tomorrow's the Day

> *It is thrifty to prepare today for the wants of tomorrow.*
> "The Ant and the Grasshopper," *Aesop's Fables*

In "Tomorrow's the Day," Corey asks that gnawing, timeless question, "Am I ready this year for Opening Day?" Invariably he is not. Corey is consoled by knowing his shortcomings are common to many who pledge loyalty to the Brotherhood of Anglers, and offers helpful hints on how to make next year different. Decide whether or not his suggestions will work for you.

An undercurrent meanders through this story: The Wife. She sits in judgement—always—in the eyes of her man who simply does not realize she is merely laughing behind his back. Rebecca West wrote, "The main difference between men and women is that men are lunatics and women are idiots." I prefer the wisdom of the greatest broad who ever walked in stilettos, Mae West, who said, "Give a man a free hand and he'll run it all over you."

Perhaps if a man gave his wife a free hand to organize his fishing things—just as she does his Sunday suit—then Opening Day might not be a last-minute nightmare of forgotten reels and torn waders. Although Corey was a lifelong bachelor, he often wrote about a wife who made up for his shortcomings and vice versa. They adored one another. Theirs was a marriage made in heaven. Corey lived vicariously through his writing, visiting himself through his words when life shortchanged him. No passage is more bittersweet than the autobiographical conclusion to his humor book, *What Every Bachelor Knows* (1961), written at the age of fifty-nine:

"Is marriage the answer? Certainly it would be a way out of the problems of being single. Perhaps I could put an advertisement in the *Marital News*, say, or the *Romance Breeders Gazette:* 'FOR SALE: One bachelor, slightly used. 1902 model, chassis still in excellent condition, original teeth and hair (what there is of it). Good on curves, and fast pickup. Complete with all accessories, including spare tire and large rear end. Any reasonable offer accepted...

"No, the habit is formed, I'm afraid. The old pipe is caked with use, the bowl is cracked and patched with adhesive tape, but it's too late to give it up now.

"And so here I am, well into my fifties, still unmarried, and it does not seem likely that I shall change. I'll go on as I am, and someday it will not matter any more whether I marry or not. And then I'll know the real advantage of being a bachelor, for there will be no family to leave behind."

Corey did die alone—with no family to leave behind. His surrogate family was a handful of friends. One was Dan Holland, a fishing editor of *Field & Stream* who authored *Trout Fishing* and other bibles of rod and reel. Dan fished with Corey throughout the world. It is fitting to dedicate the memory of that "three-pound squaretail" Corey filched on the Albany to Dan. Dan died a fortnight ago from the time I write this. He rests a stone's throw from Corey's grave in Hanover, New Hampshire overlooking Mink Brook—that secret trout stream that Corey made famous in "The Minutes of the Lower Forty."

But that's another story.

$\mathcal{T}$omorrow is the moment he's been waiting for. Tomorrow the fisherman will emerge from his annual six-months' hibernation, which began with the close of last year's trout season, and head once more for that favorite pool he has brooded about all winter. Tomorrow—rain or snow or sleet—the Law Comes Off.

Is all in readiness for the resounding clang of his alarm clock at four a.m.? Has he made good use of these idle winter months? Does he have his tackle in shape, his gear laid out, his reel oiled, his line all greased? By way of answer, let us glance into the home of a typical angler as the great event draws near....

'Tis the night before Opening Day (let Clement Moore sue me) and all through the house, not a creature is stirring except for his spouse, who has gotten up half an hour ahead to start the coffee and make some peanut butter sandwiches. His waders are hung by the chimney with care, in hopes that the patches he finally got around to gluing on last midnight will be dry by morning. His leaders are soaking overnight in the bathtub, so they will be thoroughly soft by the time he gets to the stream tomorrow and remembers where he left them. His boots are up in the attic if he could only find them, his only pair of wading socks have holes in both heels, and somebody—I said *somebody*—has deliberately mislaid his creel. His line is wound around the bedposts, his flies lie in a jumbled heap on the bedside stand, and he has collapsed on the pillow to grab a few minutes' shut-eye before his partner arrives.

Out on the lawn there arises a clatter as a jeep halts in front and his partner sounds the horn vigorously, waking everyone else in the neighborhood and eventually the fisherman himself. He springs from his bed, struggling to untangle himself from the trout line in which he has become thoroughly enmeshed. Sleepily he thrusts his right foot into the left leg of his trousers, shoves an arm through the neckband of his shirt, crams everything else in sight into his landing net, and rushes downstairs, shouting to his wife to please kindly try to recall just what in hell she did with his pipe. After a frantic search, the pipe is discovered between his teeth, where he left it last night when he went to sleep, and he hauls on his waders and starts out the front door, returning almost immediately to unhook his suspenders from the newel-post at the bottom of the stairs. The Jeep is halfway to Sullivan County before he remembers that he put his trout reel on the hall table so he would be sure to see it, his fishing jacket is still hanging on the coat rack, and he forgot to bring the peanut butter sandwiches.

"Next year," he says bitterly—because in addition he has just remembered that his license is in the pocket of the fishing jacket—"next year I won't leave everything till the last minute. Next year I'll get ready in time."

For the benefit of the repentant angler, therefore, I have listed a few things he can do to get ready for the coming trout season. If he will follow these hints carefully during the long winter months and make a point of going upstairs each night as soon dinner is over and spending the next five or six hours locked up all alone in his den, he will find that his gear is in perfect shape when Opening Day arrives. He will also find that his wife has left him and gone home to mother.

Care of Tackle

Every year a number of articles are written on the care and preservation of fishing tackle. The angler should read all these articles carefully, nodding his head from time to time and murmuring sagely: "That's a pretty good idea" or, "This fellow sure knows what he's talking about."

After reading each article, he should clip it out of the magazine and file it away in a large folder entitled "Opening Day: Things to do in preparation for." (This file will come in handy later to wrap fish in.)

One of the most important things to do in preparation for Opening Day, of course, is to sort over your collection of trout flies, and rearrange them so you can put your hands on any pattern you want without delay. To accomplish this task, some winter night turn all your fly boxes upside down and dump the contents in a heap on the tackle room table. Pour yourself a small spot of Scotch—because this job will probably take quite awhile—and paw over the assortment of flies before you. Select a number fourteen Fan Wing Cahill, hold it aloft and turn it slowly from side to side, trying to recollect where you worked it last. Let's see, now, wasn't that the fly you used to take that three-pound squaretail on the Albany, right out from under Dan Holland's nose? Place it back reverently on the pile, pour yourself another jigger of Scotch, and pick up a number twelve Quill Gordon. That would be the one you borrowed from Mac to hook that twenty-four inch grayling on Tanalian creek in Alaska. Return it to the heap on the table, fill the jigger-glass again, and pick out a small Black Gnat. Paul Clowes gave you that one, the time you took the four-pound rainbow on the North Fork of the Snake. This black-and-white fly is the one Sid Hayward tied for you out of the hair of your own bird dog. This Blue Dun is the one you used last year on the Connecticut.

Continue brooding thus over the collection, occasionally refilling your glass as you look over your favorite patterns one by one—until your wife shouts upstairs that it's three o'clock, for heaven's sakes, and aren't you ever coming to bed? Dump the flies back in the boxes and plan to sort them out tomorrow night instead. After all, you've got all winter.

Equally important in getting ready for Opening Day is to go through the pockets of your fishing jacket and remove all the superfluous items that have collected in them during the past season. There is nothing more cumbersome than a loaded fishing jacket, its sides bulging so you can barely move your arms to cast. The best way is to empty all the contents from the pockets, sort them over carefully one by one, and put back only those essential items that you could not possibly do without such as:

1. A piece of string, about ten inches long. (You never can tell when you'll need a piece of string.)

2. A hunk of copper wire. (You never know when you'll want a hunk of copper wire.)

3. A button. (You'd better keep that, because it probably came off something.)

4. A pack of stale tobacco, half full. (Might come in handy if you ever run out of tobacco.)

5. An empty tin box that you could use sometime to keep spare flies in; a red bandanna, smelling slightly of fish, in case you want to wrap something up; a bottle of fly dope with some sticky brown stuff in the bottom, in case you need to renew the prescription; a swivel, in case you ever want a swivel; a reel with the handle missing, in case you find the handle again; part of a chocolate bar, which has melted and stuck to the inside of your pocket so you can't get it out; a broken scale, which could easily be fixed; a key to something, if you could only remember what it fits; and several nice looking streamer flies with the barbs broken off, because it seems a shame to throw them away.

6. A safety pin, which you reluctantly decide to get rid of, because after all you've got to get rid of something. (Later on, when your suspenders break in the middle of the stream, you will discover that the one thing in the world you need is a safety pin.)

Repairing the Waders

Only one thing is worse than discovering at the last moment there is a hole in one leg of your waders, and that is discovering there are holes in both legs. Veteran fishermen wince at the very thought of striding across a pool and feeling their waders fill with ice-cold water. To avoid this, many fishermen fill their waders with warm water before stepping into the stream.

There are several ways of finding out whether your waders leak. One method is to fill the bathtub with water, put on your waders, and sit down in the tub. This method is not entirely satisfactory, since the immersion of a fisherman results in a corresponding displacement of water that elevates the level in the tub to a point slightly higher than the waist of the waders, causing him to assume a rather silly expression when his wife glances into the bathroom and asks him acidly just what he thinks he's doing, and wouldn't he like her to bring him one of Junior's rubber ducks?

A better method is to take the waders down into the cellar, pull them inside-out, and hang them from a couple of nails in the ceiling. Fill a bucket with water, pour it into the waders, and watch closely to see whether a leak appears. Draw another bucket of water, pour it down inside, and inspect the legs carefully. Continue to fill the waders with water until the nails in the ceiling give way, dropping the waders and flooding the cellar floor to a depth of several inches. Wade back upstairs again—quietly.

Probably the best method is to wait till you get to the stream. If there's a hole in your waders that lets the water in, cut another hole just below it to let the water out again. You'll end up just as dry as everybody else.

Preparing the Fishing Hat

The most indispensable item in any fisherman's equipment is his hat. This ancient relic—with its battered crown and well-greyed band—not only preserves the memory of every trout he ever caught, but also the smell. In case his wife ever carries out her threat to give it away to the garbage collector, the fisherman may proceed as follows: After a hasty visit to the lawyer's to institute divorce proceedings (this step is automatic), he should repair to the nearest hat store and purchase the first headgear he sees. If it does not fit, yank it down over the skull until the stitches give way so it feels better. Rip out the silk lining and hand it back to the clerk, roll the rest of the hat into a tight ball, and sit on it all the way home in order to start breaking it in. Later, as time permits, the following additional care is recommended:
1. Impregnate it thoroughly with fish slime, asafoetida, old axle grease, diesel oil, citronella, and hair tonic.
2. Festoon the band with barbed flies until it resembles a moulting hen.
3. Fill the crown with water and let it stand in the sun a few days until the seams start coming apart.

4. Place it in the driveway, crank up the garden tractor, and drive it back and forth over the hat, shoveling on an occa-sional forkful from the compost heap. Knead thoroughly.

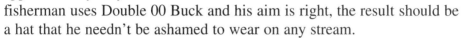

5. Last but not least, place it on a stump and shoot it with a ten-gauge magnum at approximately fifty feet. If the fisherman uses Double 00 Buck and his aim is right, the result should be a hat that he needn't be ashamed to wear on any stream.

Here, then, are a few things the prudent angler can do to get himself set for the arrival of Opening Day. Does he take advantage of the suggestions I have carefully listed above? Does he profit from his past mistakes and spend his nights over the winter to good purpose? Will he have his tackle all ready in plenty of time next year, instead of leaving everything as usual till the very last minute?

For the answer to these fascinating questions, turn back and start over again at the beginning of this article.

Two

Profile of a Trout Stream

Dan Holland retells a favorite story of Corey's in his 1949 book, *Trout Fishing*:

Corey Ford told me a very sad little story about his early days of fishing on the Beaverkill. It seems that one of the better pools was named for a fat Dutchman, not because he owned it or had any rightful claim to it, but because he had acquired a certain priority by the doubtful method of squatter's rights. This stout and sullen gentleman always fished the same pool. When he wasn't actually engaged in fishing, he sat on the bank ready to step into the water ahead of any other fisherman who might come along. The ethics of the Beaverkill don't allow anyone to enter a pool already occupied.

Corey finally had enough of these tactics and arose with the birds one morning in order to arrive at the pool first. When the gentleman in question showed up a few minutes later, Corey was tied into a nice trout and as happy as a jaybird. The Dutchman plumped himself down on the bank and watched Corey with the friendly stare of a buzzard. Corey played the trout skillfully for the benefit of his audience and, when the two-and-a-half pounder was on its side, calmly led it into the net. Then, to make sure that the man on the bank didn't miss anything, he held the net high in the air to admire the catch. About that time the bottom of the net gave way and the trout plunged back into the water. Corey sheepishly sneaked out the far side of the pool. The Dutchman, without a smile, took his place in the pool and, Corey is sure, eventually took the trout and made a pig of himself eating it.

The only moral of this story is that a trout isn't landed until it's in the frying pan.

Corey relates this episode himself in "Profile of a Trout Stream."

hey've torn down the old covered bridge at Rockland, beneath whose porcupine-chewed timbers I caught a muskrat once on a dry fly—a number fourteen Light Cahill as I recall. He was not a very large muskrat, but I had him hooked securely through an ear, and he put a permanent set in my four-ounce Thomas rod before I managed to beach him on the side of the pool. The ancient structure is gone now, replaced by an efficient steel span; but the pool is still there, and the dark, lovely run below it, and the succeeding miles of foaming swirls and fast eddies that have made the Beaverkill—for me, at least—the best-loved fishing water of them all.

I suppose it's *the* historic American trout stream. Generations of anglers have floundered through its rapids, and stepped over their waders in its cold deep holes, and hung up their backcasts in the balsams along its banks. Leading sportsmen from all over the world have come to whip its legendary pools. The record brook trout in New York State, eight-and-a-half pounds, was taken in one of its tributaries. It was here in the Catskills that the art of dry fly-tying was born in America, some sixty years ago, when Theodore Gordon crested the famous Quill that bears his name. Many of our other popular patterns—the Hendrickson and the Fan Wing Royal and the Female Beaverkill were designed to imitate the insects hatching along the Beaverkill's grassy banks.

I was born on the Beaverkill myself, in a manner of speaking. I learned to cast a dry fly over Barnhart's Pool, under the choleric instruction of Ted Townsend, the old master. I've fished many hundred streams since, but to this day, whenever I look down on a promising bit of water in Canada or Alaska, I find myself comparing it with Barnhart's, or Junction Pool, or Cain's. They're all still there, the fine old pools with names that fall like music on the ear: Barrel Pool, Henrickson's, Horse Brook Run, and School House Rocks, where at night the big browns still make a meal of the dace in the riffles. Mountain Pool, Wagon Wheel Pool, Cemetery Pool, and Painter's Bend, where I saw Ted Townsend land a five-pound brook by moonlight on a number eighteen Black Gnat. The Forks at Roscoe, and Ferdon's Eddy, and Desbrow's Pool—named after Roscoe's dour undertaker who used to rise before dawn each morning and stake his claim in the center of his favorite stretch, fending off all intruders by casting his fly vigorously in their general direction. Once, when Desbrow was summoned to Roscoe to conduct the obsequies for a prominent citizen who had thoughtlessly died in the middle of fishing season, I sneaked into his pool and managed to hook at two-pound squaretail just as "Dezzy" returned, panting, to the stream. Before his apoplectic gaze, I scooped up the trout in my net and held it aloft for him to see. The strands of the net gave way, the trout fell back into the current and was instantly whisked out of sight. I made my way to the bank without a word, and Dezzy stalked past me triumphantly and took his place in the middle of the pool. For all I know, he's still there.

The stream has changed since the good old days, of course. The fishing isn't what it used to be, they tell you today. When I first fished the Beaverkill over twenty-five years ago, they told me sadly: "The fishing nowadays isn't what it was." I suppose that when Hendrick Hudson sailed up to the Catskills the Indians told him: "You should have discovered this place a hundred years ago. That's when the fishing was really good." It doesn't matter: A trout stream is more than the fish in it. A great trout stream like the Beaverkill is a legend, a fly book filled with memories, a part of the lives of all the devoted anglers, living or dead, who ever held a taut line in its current. A generation from now, I have no doubt, they'll still be standing on the same rocks and hammering the same pools and climbing back up the bank with the same empty creels and the same insistent alibis: The water was too high. The water was too low. It was too hot. It was too cold. It was too bright. It was too dark. The fishing isn't what it used to be...

This wide-placed river, flowing westward through New York State to join the East Branch of the Delaware near the Pennsylvania border, has led a tumultuous life. It was born in humble surroundings in the heart of the Catskills, just west of Slide Mountain. A mere freshnet, it left home at an early age and worked its determined way south, cascading down the mountainside on its slippery bottom, foraging across the boggy meadows, feeding hungrily on every spring hole and trickle. By the time it crossed into Sullivan County, it had grown to be a brawling brook—it fought under the name of Little Beaverkill—that could take on any angler and throw him in its strong current. It wrestled its way south in a series of swift falls, past the towns of Beaverkill and Rockland down to Roscoe. There it met the gentle Willowemoc, an attractive trout stream from the east, and their romance was consummated in a happy marriage of waters at Junction Pool. The Willowemoc gracefully surrendered its identity,

ərkill, a broad and mature river now, settled down con-
ɔral meadows to raise its prolific family of brook trout
ɪbows.

ⅼɑɪ trout stream, with much of its watershed still protected by
ɪɔrest cover, and underlain by a rock formation favorable to water
conservation. Its source is at 2,860 feet, and the average rate of fall is
about forty-two feet per mile, making its course just swift enough. There
are no ponds, artificial or otherwise, and no falls or dams that would be a
barrier to fish. In all but the lowest stretch, the stream temperature is
suitable for browns and rainbows, and the upper mileage is cold enough
to support squaretails all summer. The bottom is strewn with blocky
boulders, which offer good shelter for trout, and an abundance of small
feeder tributaries, such as Russell and Berry Brooks, provide natural
nursery streams.

Probably the outstanding reason that the Beaverkill achieved its fame
is the fantastic amount of insect life that flourishes along its course each
May and June. I have never seen such hatches of flies along a trout
stream, before or since. There was usually a smaller hatch in the morning, I remember, but the great hatches used to occur between four and six
of an evening. Avid anglers would patrol the stream in shifts all afternoon, as far down as Cooks Falls, waiting to spot the first telltale insects
moving upstream. You could always tell when a hatch was about to
begin. A car would streak along the road, a breathless fisherman would
race up the porch-steps to awaken his slumbering partner and snatch a
pair of waders from the hook by the door. As the magic word spread,
more and more anglers would pour out of their lodgings, struggling into
fishing jackets and shouldering creels as they ran. Within minutes, the
whole placid valley would be boiling with activity as excited fishermen
braked their cars beside the stream in a spurt of gravel, scrambled past
each other down the bank, and waded out into their chosen pools, rod in
hand, ready for the fateful moment.

You waited there in ominous silence. The stream flowed past you quietly with nary a rise to mar its smooth, untroubled surface. The sun was
setting and the waning lemon light glinted on the wings of a couple of
large, dun-colored flies drifting lazily in the air. Another fly appeared,
and then several more; they seemed to come mysteriously from nowhere;
all at once the sky overhead was filled with them. They beat upstream

horizontally like snowflakes driven by a gale, fluttering against your face, zigzagging heavily down, down toward the water, flopping exhausted at last onto the stream. As they lit, the quiet pool exploded abruptly with hungry trout. There seemed to be a fish for every fly. A great brown rose before you; as you cast to it, a big brook turned at your feet; a couple of monsters struck simultaneously at an insect just behind you. The blizzard of flies continued to swirl past you, the pool bubbled and seethed as though someone were tossing handfuls of pebbles into the stream, the splashes of breaking trout mingled with the skirl of your reel and the song of your tight line cutting across the current in the final dusk.

I don't know to this day which insects made up the biggest hatches. Some say they were Mayflies; other insist they were Coffin Flies; still others argue they were Stones. The controversy still rages among old-timers. Most of them incline to the belief that they were Stones, perhaps out of deference to Art Tyler, of Livingston Manor, who claimed he used an artificial Stone to take that ten-and-a-quarter pound, thirty-inch brown near Elk Brook on May 17, 1930. On the other hand, I remember a four-and-a-half pound brown in the icebox at Ferdon's that was definitely taken on a Yellow May. I know. I was on the other end of the line.

*M*y fishing partner in those days was the only man I have ever known who could fall into a stream clear over his head and come up again with his pipe still going. We always stayed at Ferdon's, a rambling, friendly boarding house on the bank of the Beaverkill, just above the famous pool that bears its name. Ferdon's catered to fishermen. There were nails along the clapboard of the front porch on which to rest your rod at night, and you could hang your waders over the railing to dry and take off your wet pants in the living room and wring out your socks in the fireplace. Somehow, whenever I write a fishing story, I always seem to be describing Ferdon's: the smoke-filled upstairs bedroom with our freshly greased enameled line draped over the chandelier and our boots comfortably crossed on the white counterpane as we oiled our reels; the spacious icebox with its individual pans of trout, each marked with the owner's name; the dining room where we lingered over coffee to tell about the ones that got away: "Here I had him right up to the net. He'd have gone five pounds, maybe six—I wouldn't have been surprised if he went seven or even eight..."

It was at Ferdon's that I first came to know Ted Townsend, the fabled game warden of Westchester County—a violent, opinionated, profane, wonderful man—the most complete angler I have ever known. Ted was a true artist with the dry fly. He could catch a trout when there wasn't one there. I've seen him do it. He would stand beside a deep run and float his fly down over it patiently, forty or fifty times, until some slumbering squaretail, peering up blearily at the succession of tidbits passing over-head, would concluded that the evening hatch had begun ahead of time and would rouse himself to strike at Ted's lure on the fifty-first cast.

Ted tied his own flies, of course, usually right on the bank. He would arrive streamside with a long butterfly net in which he would capture the several insects hovering over the water. Then he would repair to a nearby rock, spread out the specimens beside him, and consider them thoughtful-ly for a while. Once he had made up his mind which succulent insect seemed to be the Chef's Special of the day, he would open the large sewing basket he always carried, take out a small vise, scissors, spools of varicolored silk thread, skeins of wool, peacock hurl, tinsel, and assorted feathers, and skillfully fashion a facsimile of the fly so accurate that it would fool me, let alone the fish. Ted was always a stickler for color, insisting that a trout could detect the slightest difference in shades. In support of this argument, he liked to cite an experience he had a few years back when he stopped at a stationery store in Liberty and, more or less out of kindness to the proprietor, purchased three very old and faded Royal Coachmen that had been standing in the window so long that the sun had bleached their red windings to a vague pink. That afternoon, when no other fisherman on the stream was able to raise so much as a chub, Ted's three odd-colored Coachmen did a rushing business until dark. "It isn't the fish who are color-blind," Ted used to goad, "It's the goddam fishermen."

In addition to his other accomplishments, Ted added a new refinement to the angling art: He employed a trout spotter. While I would sit on the bank of the stream smoking, Ted's loyal partner, Melly, would cruise up and down the highway in an open car, peering at the various pools through his binoculars. Whenever he detected a rise, he would race back upstream, honk the horn violently, and bellow down to us, "Hurry up!

Quick! I saw one come up twice down at Cook's Falls!" Ted would drive back with him and take the trout, lead it to the net, and then gently release it. I never knew anyone who loved the sport more. Ted has gone now to the Happy Fishing Grounds, but I am confident at this moment that he is using a golden harpstring for a leader and casting a Fan Wing Royal tied with white feathers plucked from his wings.

ed Townsend was part of a great tradition that began in this country in 1890 when Theodore Gordon, the leading American angling authority of his time, received a packet of dry flies from the great English angler, F.M. Halford. Each fly was carefully identified in Halford's own handwriting with appropriate flourishes, and his accompanying letter stated: "I can quite imagine that in some parts of your country fish could be taken with dry fly where the more usual sunk fly would be of no avail. My difficulty, however, as to advising you of patterns likely to be successful is chiefly due to the fact that I have no knowledge of the streams or lakes nor of the genera and species of natural flies prevalent in them...Knowing your own rivers, you can select the patterns which seem likely, and dress them yourself."

Thus the dry fly winged across the Atlantic to the New World and settled on the Beaverkill to stay. One of Gordon's first improvisations on the Halford patterns was the Quill Gordon—long my own favorite trout fly—of which he wrote modestly: "The Quill is a very troublesome fly on account of its hackle, but as a dry fly it is typical of certain ephemera and I have had some remarkable experiences with it."

The Beaverkill Club and the Brooklyn Fly Fishing Club own sections of the stream that are closed to non-members; but, since they control and stock these waters regularly, the posted areas serve as valuable reservoirs of trout that benefit the entire stream. Besides, it's always more fun when there are a few closed sections of a stream into which an amateur poacher can slip his fly now and then. Some of my most enjoyable moments were had when I used to sneak into the forbidden water of Russel Brook, presided over by an obdurate old fellow. I wonder how many times I have torn my waders scrambling over the barbed wire in headlong retreat pursued by his irate cries.

Another favorite poaching preserve of mine, as I recall, was the deep run just below a forbidding stone mansion on the Little Beaverkill known as Craigie Clair. There was always something of a mystery about Craigie Clair. Rumor had it that the sole occupant was a beautiful but demented young girl who used to let down her golden hair from an upstairs window and lure unwary anglers into her granite castle for what probably amounted to nothing worse than an afternoon's pleasant seduction. I fished past Craigie Clair, hopefully, a number of times, but I never got lured. Maybe I wasn't her type.

No, the fishing isn't what it used to be. The current is faster, it seems to me, and the rocks are slipperier when you step up on them. It's farther to the other side of the stream these days, and they've added a couple of bends in the river that I never noticed before. The bank is higher when you try to climb back to your car. And the kind of leaders they're putting out nowadays are so fine you have to hold them farther and farther away to see them, and it's getting harder to make out these modern flies on the water.

The fishermen may change, but the Beaverkill never grows old, anymore than a legend can age, or a song. New fishermen will arrive each year to spot its rises and wade its rapids and explore its deep swift runs for the first time: "There's a likely looking pool, now. Barnhart's, I hear it's called. I wonder if anybody ever fished it before. Maybe I'm the first ever to put my fly over that fast eddy behind the rock..."

Look out, young man. Watch your backseat; the ghosts of a hundred departed anglers are standing behind you. That pool you are entering was once the favorite fishing hole of John Tainter Foote. Ted Townsend used to perch atop that very rock on which you are standing now. Perhaps Theodore Gordon dropped his first Quill over that same dark eddy where you have just cast your fly.

Good luck, young man, and good fishing. I hope you take that big old brown that lies below the boulder. I've been trying for him myself for twenty-five years.

Three

The Great Indoors

Helpful Hints for Sportsmen by an Expert Who Has Spent Twenty Years in the Woods, Most of Them Trying to Find His Way Out Again

*A*nyone can learn to tie a dry fly. All you need is patience, perseverance, and a couple of extra fingers on each hand. It also helps to have three thumbs.

The basic principle of fly-tying is to create a likeness of the natural insect on the water. Trout feed on a varied diet including flies, grasshoppers, small crustaceans, larvae, nymphs, and other unpleasant-looking quarry that I'd just as soon not go into here; and the sportsman must imitate these items in order to fool the fish.

Before attempting to tie a fly, the angler should make a careful study of the living organisms in the pool he intends to fish. For this purpose, I recommend a long-handled dip net with a fine wire-mesh bag. By dragging this along the bottom of the pool, he will bring up an interesting assortment of insects, rusted tin cans, a half grapefruit rind, and part of an old rubber boot. In addition, if he is lucky, he will dip up a good trout, thus saving himself the trouble of tying a fly in order to catch one.

The actual choice of pattern is up to the individual. Some fishermen try to tie a fly that will please the fish. This is obviously silly, because nobody knows what a fish really likes. Anything that spends its whole life swimming underwater, of all places, is bound to have peculiar tastes. The best plan is to tie a fly that pleases the fisherman, since, after all, he is the one who is going to use it. I usually employ a favorite pattern of my own invention that has celluloid wings and an electric light in the eye and that I can wind up with a key. The fact that I've never caught anything with it only proves what I was saying about fish.

It is not necessary for the amateur fly-tier to own an elaborate outfit. All he requires is a few simple tools such as a vise, magnifying glass, mirror, embroidery scissors, forceps, lance, button-hook, fly-tying wax, cement, shellac-varnish, thread clips, bobbin, bodkin (or female bobbin), and an assortment of various colored threads and several trunkfuls of feathers. The alert angler will increase his feather collection from time to time by: a) pilfering them from sofa-cushions; b) plucking them from the neck of his neighbor's prize rooster; or c) filching them from the Easter bonnet of the lady sitting just ahead in church. This method will produce some colorful plumes, as well as a poke in the nose from the lady's husband.

Now for the technique itself. The first step is to secure a large hook so you can see what you're doing and place it in a vise like this. No, I guess it's the other end that goes in the vise. *There* we are. Now tighten the vise securely and tie off the head of the hook with a whip-finish knot, taking care, of course, not to drop the spool of thread under the table as I seem to have done. Would you mind moving a little? I think it's caught around your ankle. Thank you very much. Now I'll just finish the knot by cutting off the end with a razor blade. Well, I seem to have cut the wrong thread, but maybe if I sort of wind it around the hook a couple of times it will hold all right.

Now we'll go through our collection of feathers here and pick out a good hackle. Will somebody shut the window, please? They're blowing all over the floor. Grasp the tip of the hackle firmly and spread it by pulling the fibers against the grain back to the butt. Oooops, I pulled a little too hard that time, but I guess there's enough of it left to wind around the hook a couple of times. I don't understand why it keeps coming unwound again, but I'll fix it with some of this cement if I could get the...cork out of the...ugh! That's all right, I was planning to send these clothes to the cleaners anyway. Now then, has anybody seen that hackle? That's funny, it must be somewhere...I had it a moment ago. Oh, here it is, stuck to the seat of my pants. Well, never mind, we can put the hackle on later.

Next we come to the wings, which after all, are the most important part of a dry fly. Select a good stout tail feather, yank out a couple of hunks of webbing, and arrange them side-by-side on the shank of the hook, holding them in place with the forefinger. Spread a loop of thread with the third and fourth fingers of one hand; pass the loop over the wings with the fifth finger of the other hand; pull it tight with the sixth finger of the third hand. Now all that remains is to figure out how to remove your forefinger without taking the whole fly apart again.

And now if the rest of you will follow these instruction carefully, I'll dig up a couple of nightcrawlers and wait for you out on the stream.

– Four –

My Namesake

*Recording the sensations of a devout angler upon
becoming the proud godfather of a new trout fly*

In "Profile of a Trout Stream," Corey lavishes praise and indulges in nostalgia for his beloved Beaverkill River; in "My Namesake," he reinforces that affection. In the previous chapter, Corey makes a mockery of himself regarding his utter ineptitude for tying flies. Imagine his rapture, then, upon learning a trout fly has been named for him—and that future casts upon the sacred pools of the Beaverkill by untold fishermen might be whipped with a Corey Ford Fly. In "My Namesake," Corey doesn't try to mask his elation—nor his scorn for the bait fisherman.

It seems I have arrived at last. After all these years, I have finally crashed the Hall of Fame; and now there is nothing left to live for. I belong, it appears, to the Ages.

I will admit that, up to now, I had not been conspicuously slated for Posterity. On the other hand, I had come to feel pretty much neglected by the Admissions Committee of Valhalla. Fame, it seemed to me, had been rather consistently giving me the runaround. I had never, for example, been tapped for a toothpaste ad. I had never been invited for a blindfold test. I had never had a mountain named for me by Commander Byrd. (To be sure, there is said to be a Ford Range at the South Pole, but it is probably some other Mr. Ford.) I had never endorsed a mattress, cold cream, or yeast; I had never had a theater named in my honor; I was not even the godfather of a Reuben's Sandwich.

Now all that is forgiven and forgotten. Now I don't care about my failure to endorse a mattress or christen a boat. Commander Byrd can keep his mountains. I have scaled a higher summit of fame than all of these. At last I have reached the peak of ambition. I have just had a trout fly named after me.

This spectacular discovery was made just now while I was in the act of glancing quite leisurely through the 1931 Fishing Catalogue of that excellent craftsman and purveyor of trout flies to their majesties, the anglers of the Beaverkill—Mr. Walter Dette of Roscoe, New York. Each year, Mr. Dette prepares for his loyal customers a complete list of his latest and best creations, both the orthodox patterns and one or two new models of his own invention that he has tied over the long winter, with consummate skill, to meet the varied and exacting demands of the fishing fraternity the following spring. (The trout, it appears, are not so particular.) Yesterday, in the annual burst of preseasonal fishing fever that litters my room the first week every April with fresh-varnished rods and uncoiled line and leaders soaking in tumblers of water, I chanced to browse absently through this tantalizing pamphlet, mentally weighing the merits of a Light Cahill and a Wickham's Fancy, or recalling that particular pool on the Beaverkill where I would drop a Fan Wing Coachman someday exactly at dusk; and as I read down the list, I came abruptly upon the following startling item, located significantly between the Gold Ribbed Hare's Ear and the Cowdung:

> 101. Corey Ford: Grey Body; Grey Tail; Blue-Grey Hackle; Cream Hackle-Point Wing . . . .$3.00 per doz.

At first, I must confess, this description came as a bit of a shock. I may have worn grey tails once or twice, at morning weddings; but as far as I know, my body is of the conventional pink and despite the fact that I shave myself and the light in my bathroom is pretty bad, "Blue-grey hackle" seemed to be going a bit too far. Moreover, if anyone had come up to me on the street and so much as suggested that I had cream-colored wings, and could be had for three dollars a dozen, I'd have given him a poke in the nose. After all, I have my pride.

It was only after a second and more sober reading that the full significance of unexpected canonization burst upon me. At last, it appears, I have made the grade. At last, after years of earnest apprenticeship in the art of the dry fly, I have been admitted formally to the exclusive order of the Brothers of the Angle. Now perhaps I can claim some mild kinship with such famed and slightly mythical masters of the art of fishing as Zane Grey or Dr. Van Dyke or G.M.L. La Branche or F. Gray Griswold or George Parker Holden. Now I can hold up my head a little in the presence of expert anglers such as Ted Townsend and Courtney Riley Cooper and Van Campden Heilner. Now I can still maintain a little self-respect even when my fishing partner pulls a five-pound rainbow from the very pool that I have whipped two hours in vain. I may not be any good, but I bet my trout fly is.

It is a rare order, this secret and solemn fraternity of the dry fly. The initiation into it is slow, and the successive degrees are difficult for the layman to understand. Every year, for example, there arises the same to-do and discussion regarding the comparative merits of the Dry Fly vs the Worm—as if there were any comparison. I have no brief against the worm fisherman. I do think it might be a little easier on the rest of us if the state would simply give him the money to go down to Fulton Market and pick out the fish he wants instead of making him spend a hard day dredging a stream with a steel pole and bait; but I like to think that every worm fisherman has the makings of an angler in him, provided the right influence were brought to bear.

As far as debating the comparative merits of the two lures, however, dry fly fishermen will admit at once that it is almost invariably easier to get fish with a worm. If the object of your fishing is to get fish, then use worms or dynamite, or pull them out with your hands; but if, instead, the object of your fishing is sport, if you desire the thrill of pitting your wits against the instinct of a wary trout, if you wish the satisfaction of a cast well-made and a fly safely delivered over the nose of a rising brown, if you long for the lunge and swirl and the sudden terrifying leap of a rainbow at the end of your line, then that is something else again. You do not ask the golfer, for example, why he bothers to knock the ball over the green with a clumsy knobbed stick, when it would be so much easier for him if he just picked up the ball and dropped it into the hole with his hands. You do not ask the hunter why he scorns to shoot a sitting bird. After all, there is no argument: Either you are a dry fly fisherman, or you can kindly get the hell out of my pool.

It is on the Beaverkill—where I was initiated many years ago and am forever getting the hook caught in my long white beard—that this art of the dry fly has perhaps reached the height of sophistication. Ferdon's excellent River View Inn at Roscoe, when the Mayfly hatch is on, approaches the intense efficiency of mobilization camp. During the long day, anglers in Martian-like waders drive their cars up and down the ten-mile stretch of road from Roscoe to Cook's Falls, patrolling the tranquil, sun-specked river and marking their special pools for the night's offensive. Perhaps they nap a little in the heat of the afternoon, exchange experiences of their efforts during the early morning, discuss the approaching evening's hatch—"ought to be due between seven and eight tonight." By four or five, they commence to wander away from the Inn in secret groups of two or three, climbing quietly into their cars and driving innocently around the turn of the road, and then speeding hell-bent for election toward their chosen rendezvous down the river. By six o'clock, dim, brown-clad figures have wandered out into the various pools of the broad stream and staked their claims for the evening's sport, for that rigid code of ethics that still exists in sport—even if it is to be found nowhere else in America—forbids another angler on pain of ostracism to trespass upon a pool has that has thus been claimed.

Six-thirty, seven—the patient figure at the head of the pool makes a few tentative casts and waits. His partner, below him, lights a pipe, and the flare of the match is pink in the increasing dusk. The night train thunders along the embankment bound toward Roscoe, and the engineer leans out of the window and waves amiably.

Seven-thirty. The angler is scanning the darkening sky. A few small objects are speeding upstream, high overhead, like leaves borne by an invisible wind. As he watches, the dots grow thicker and thicker, driving in a steady blizzard of grey snowflakes against the night sky. Below him, to the right, there is a splash; a smaller fish has leapt for an insect that hovered too near the surface. It is the invitation to the dance. Now a more solid chunk above galvanizes him to attention; now the water about him is suddenly filled with activity as the flies commence to drop lower and skitter helplessly along the fast current. He strains his eyes and peers at the smooth, black stretch of fast water beneath the willows at the bank. There is a silent bump on the surface and a few flecks of foam. Now his rod is whipping silently, the line feeding out through the agate guides as he measures his distance. He shoots his fly forward and checks the cast in time so that the line falls upon the current in an upstream curve, the fly riding serenely, directly over the spot where the bump in the water was seen. He retrieves the line below him in the darkness and casts it upstream again. The fly rides past him once more and then abruptly the water breaks, a green shoulder turns as the fly disappears, he tightens his line slowly and then strikes....

Ten o'clock that night. The water-soaked waders are stacked at last on the back porch of the Inn, the rods are laid reverently upon convenient brackets, the day's catch is heaped in tin pans in Mrs. Ferdon's spacious icebox. Upstairs the tired anglers in stocking feet gather in Fred's room, or Bill's, floundering exhausted across the bed, pulling corks, raising glasses exultantly as they toast their success, or reveal at last the secrets they had guarded so carefully during the afternoon.

"I just had a hunch to try the Cemetery Pool tonight..."

"I seen this morning where there was a funny fly with a bright blue body and brown wings so I tied one just to try, and..."

They have now plugged the stream all day and brought home a creel loaded with small fish just within the law. They have fished at most a couple of hours, and their catch may be one trout, or two. But they have tasted the true joy of angling—the expert art of the dry fly.

This is the fraternity, then, to which I like to feel that I now belong. I like to picture the Corey Ford Fly (grey body, blue-grey hackle, cream hackle-point wings, tied in sizes from six to fourteen, three dollars per doz., address Walter Dette, Roscoe, New York) being used on the

Beaverkill by these masters of the art. I like to think of my name being cursed by some angler on the Aesopus or the Willowemoc who has just embedded his hook in the high branches of a dead hemlock over the stream. I should like to see my namesake played over the waters of the Restigouche (and, incidentally, if any plutocratic owner of a section of that highly restricted Nirvana of all anglers should ever take it into his head to invite my partner and myself to try our luck on his stream this May or June, he will find that I am practically a pushover for an invitation and will guarantee to throw in a dozen Corey Ford Flies into the bargain). I should like to try it again myself in that pool above Juniper on the Miramichi, or in Fish Creek in Wyoming, or in the Jacques Cartier River in the beautiful and well-stocked Laurentides Park north of Quebec.

Mr. Dette, it appears, has succeeded in manufacturing a Corey Ford Fly. There is one other request I have to make—if he would only manage somehow to manufacture a Corey Ford trout that can be guaranteed to always take this lure, my satisfaction will be complete.

– Five –

Yankee Rod-Maker

In this piece, Corey pays tribute to a century-old firm of favorite rod- and fly-makers. A half-century has passed since he proclaimed his admiration in "Yankee Rod-Maker." Since then, Orvis has become a household word, synonymous with the best in American fly rods, reels, and accessories. Many fine makers of angling equipment populate the market today. However, there is something constant about a company such as Orvis, which has stood the test of time while serving the needs of the fisherman, whether he casts his line in the Battenkill or in the Volga. It's called tradition.

In the pleasant, elm-shaded Vermont village of Manchester, hidden on a side street off Route 7 that bisects the town, is a white frame building that is the mecca of trout fishermen from all over the nation. Once it was a tin shop, when the industry flourished in these parts. Now its cellar is stacked with bundles of imported Tonkin cane; fresh-glued sections of split bamboo dry in the curing ovens; in the low-ceilinged workshops on the first floor, local artisans put on the ferrules and bind the guides to produce what is probably the finest fly rod made in America today.

Ninety-eight years ago, a Manchester pharmacist and innkeeper named Charles F. Orvis turned out a few bamboo rods in his spare time for his friends to use on the nearby Battenkill River. Their reputation spread; eventually he gave up his drugstore and hotel and founded the tackle company that still bears his name. The Yankee ingenuity and the personal satisfaction in fine craftsmanship have not changed in a century. Superintendent Wes Jordan will lead you proudly past skilled workmen who slit the cane into six carefully calibrated triangular strips, tapered to a fine point, and cement them together to form a solid hexagonal shaft. He will show you the drying room, the silk-winding process, the way the

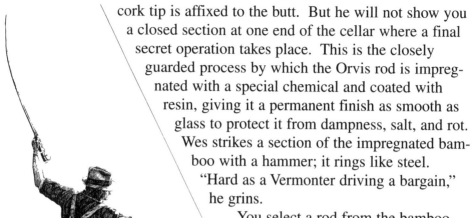

cork tip is affixed to the butt. But he will not show you a closed section at one end of the cellar where a final secret operation takes place. This is the closely guarded process by which the Orvis rod is impregnated with a special chemical and coated with resin, giving it a permanent finish as smooth as glass to protect it from dampness, salt, and rot. Wes strikes a section of the impregnated bamboo with a hammer; it rings like steel.

"Hard as a Vermonter driving a bargain," he grins.

You select a rod from the bamboo thicket of finished products in the showroom, and Duckie Corkran, the genial president of the company, fits it with an imported reel and a tapered line of the right weight. You step out onto the lawn, in the bright Vermont sunshine, and lengthen your cast across the grass to make sure the rod is right for you. You're doing more than buying a rod; you are stepping back a hundred years to experience a pride in workmanship that was part of the earliest New England tradition, and which still flourishes in this small Vermont town.

Upstairs, in a little room as casual and cozy as a New England parlor, sits Hallie Galaise of Manchester, one of the world's outstanding woman fly-tiers. Hallie joined the Orvis company forty-three years ago when she was fourteen. She has been fashioning feathered trout and salmon lures ever since, and she can tie any one of 2,200 separate and distinct patterns on request. She ties in the English fashion, without using a vise, holding the shank of the tiny hook between her bee's-waxed fingers, and whipping silk and hackle nimbly into a delicate Royal Coachman or a Light Cahill, while she rocks back and forth and chats with the customer as nonchalantly as a housewife with her knitting. Like a true artist, she makes it look so easy.

Take along the rod you have picked out. Try it for brown trout in the Battenkill, where the first Orvis rods were used. Whip it over the rainbow waters of the upper Connecticut River north of Colebrook in New Hampshire, or the salmon lakes of Maine: Sebago and Moosehead and

Rangely. Wherever you use it—and you'll find Orvis rods as far east as Newfoundland, and west to British Columbia—you'll be holding something in your hand that is part of New England itself, as strong and straight and durable as the Vermonter who made it.

– Six –

I'll Fish Again Yesterday

Corey often refers to the "Brotherhood of the Angle," and in the previous stories you get a keen sense of the kinship among fishermen and the respect they share for their sport. In this story, the Brotherhood reflects something else—a kind of spirituality. For fishing isn't just the right lure in the right stream at the right time: It's the closeness one feels—the abused phrase "communing with Nature" comes to mind—but yes, it is just that. When a dedicated fisherman is in a beautiful place, alone, casting a line into dark trout pools, he or she takes up a silent conversation with something rather holy. When that sanctity is broken or defamed, to some—such as Corey—the purity of the sport is sorely violated, as here in "I'll Fish Again Yesterday."

I could close my eyes and see it all again. The stream made a bend to the right, I remembered, and there was a long slick pool, and below it was a boulder shaped like a coffeepot. No, come to think of it, the boulder must have been at the head of the pool, because the stream parted around it and the main channel ran dark and deep along the far bank, and that was where Old Faithful had risen to my fly.

I called him Old Faithful because he had been rising regularly every hour on the hour, and I had been trying for him for three days. I had offered him every pattern in my book and a few others I made up on the spot. I had worked him in the early morning with a Black Gnat, and in the evening with a White Miller, and once, when it was almost dark, he had turned under a Spent Wing Cahill, but I retrieved the fly too soon. And then on the morning of the fourth day, I had tied on a number sixteen Quill Gordon, my favorite fly, and made a long cast so that the fly lit on the grass above the bank and fell lightly onto the slick, and he sucked it in.

He had come clear out of the water as I lifted the rod, and for a moment I had a picture of him hanging there in space, the fly embedded in his lower jaw and the leader slanting down to the stream. Everything was immobilized at that instant, when my mind clicked the shutter: the great trout suddenly rigid at the height of his leap, a few shining drops of water still suspended in the air; a blue heron halted in mid-flight with its disjointed wings bent backward like a Siamese dancer; a marmot frozen on the bank in an attitude of permanent horror. That was the picture I had carried in my mind for—how long was it?—twenty years.

So now, twenty years later, I was going back to fish the stream again. I had never told anyone where it was, of course. A man may share his wealth, or his liquor, or the names in his address book; but there are some things—a pet grouse cover, a favorite piece of trout water—that he does not tell. All these years I had remembered it as the finest dry fly stream in America. I had flown two thousand miles to find the coffeepot boulder, to drop a fly once more on the secret pool that no one knew about except myself.

I rented a car at the airport, and as I drove south, the sagebrush hills unrolled before me in a familiar pattern. I had not bothered to bring a map; the white Tetons stood against the sky, and I knew where I was going. The bumpy road wound through the foothills and crossed a narrow bridge, and there would be a little country store and gas pump on the left. Across the road, under some pine, would be a few log cabins for rent. The cabin where I used to stay was on the very bank of the stream, and at night after supper I used to wade out into the flat stretch beside it, when the evening hatch was on, and see the concentric circles of rising rainbows everywhere. I never met any other fishermen. Muskrats scurried silently up and down the banks, and once I watched a cow moose browsing on the opposite shore, her head underwater to the nape of her neck.

The Tetons were looming larger ahead, and I was beginning to wonder. The road was smoother that I remembered it, and very straight. Instead of skirting a hill, it plunged right through, leaving a wake of uprooted stumps and tumbled earth. Now and then, looking down from a high embankment, I could see a section of the abandoned road below me, winding off through the trees in search of a less efficient and more leisurely past. Cars zoomed by me, but I drove slowly, looking for the little store and gas pump. Maybe this new highway would miss it altogether. Then before I knew it I was crossing the bridge—a wide concrete one now—and I halted beside the finest dry fly stream in America.

There were no cabins under the pines. In their place was a modern double-decker motel, and behind it the trees had been cleared to make room for a sizable trailer camp. Across the highway, where the country store had been, was an up-to-date shopping center the length of a city block, with its own post office, garage, butcher shop, supermarket, restaurant, and glass-fronted bar with neon lights. Cars were parked fender to fender, and I had some trouble finding a vacant slot at the far end. I walked back along the paved sidewalk, elbowing my way past women vacationers in slacks, and entered a door marked "Rental Office."

The man behind the counter told me I was lucky. There was only one room left tonight, on the second floor of the motel. This was the height of the fishing season, he reminded me, and "people us'ally make their reservations way ahead. First time you're here?"

I explained that I had been here a long time ago, before the war.

"I guess you'll notice a lot of improvements since then," he said, as I paid for my room in advance. "It's been a big development of this stream."

He turned to ring up the cash register, and I stole a glance at the fishing equipment around me. A number of shellacked wooden poles were stacked in a corner, and the walls were hung with long-handled dip nets, metal gaffs, and minnow buckets. On the shelf above the counter was a complete assortment of spoons and plugs, spinning tackle, lead sinkers, jars of salmon eggs, and a small tray of artificial lures, mostly grasshoppers and rubber hellgramites. The showcase was filled with souvenir ashtrays, decorated with trout, and a revolving rack offered a selection of comic postcards showing fat anglers falling in the water or catching mermaids. "How's the fishing?" I asked, pocketing my change.

"Oh, they been taking quite a few," the man behind the counter said, "up to eight or ten inches. That's the size the state is stocking now."

It was late afternoon, and there was still time for me to make the evening hatch. I changed to my waders and hurried down to the stream, along a gravel path bordered with cut logs. It led past the trailer camp to the flat stretch I used to fish at night after supper. The bank was lined with people plopping spinning lures from shore, and I could see the silhouettes of more fishermen along the concrete bridge, dangling their hooks below. Children scurried up and down the bank, tossing out sticks for a dog to fetch, and on the opposite side of the stream, where I had watched the cow moose once, a middle-aged woman was washing her hair. Her neck was craned over the water, and a trail of white suds drifted below her in the slow current.

I thought I saw a rise, although it might have been a pebble tossed by one of the children, and I waded out toward it. A couple of paper cups and a crumpled cellophane cigarette wrapper bobbed downstream past me; the evening hatch had started. As I lengthened my line, I heard the steady thudding of an outboard motor, and a rowboat rounded the point with three men and woman trolling in its wake. They passed directly over the spot where I had seen the rise, and waved to me cordially.

I reeled in again, waded ashore, and strolled back up the path to the bar.

All the tables were taken, so I planted a felt-soled wading shoe on the brass rail. The television set behind the bar was broadcasting a quiz program, and a jukebox across the room blasted a rival rock-and-roll. The tune was familiar, but I couldn't place it for the moment. A young man in rubber knee-boots was standing beside me, his elbows hooked on the counter. He noticed my waders and sidled closer, drawn by a common bond of brotherhood. "Catch anything?" he asked me.

I shook my head. It was hard to talk above all the noise.

"I got one the other day," he volunteered, "went better'n a pound."

I nodded absently. I had just recognized the tune on the jukebox; it was called "Tea for Two Cha-Cha." They had been playing the same tune twenty years ago. My companion was saying something, and I bent my head toward him. "I'm sorry, I didn't hear you."

"...have on," he repeated, his lips beside my ear. "What were ya using?"

"Fly!" I shouted back.

"And now for five hundred dollars, Mrs. Nussbaum," the quizmaster on the television screen was asking, "can you name three Presidents of the United States with beards?"

"Flies ain't any good around here," my brother angler confided. "I tell ya what ya wanna use, if ya wanna catch a big one." He looked around to make sure he was not overheard, a somewhat unnecessary precaution, and placed a fraternal hand on my shoulder. "This is just between us, see."

"...and two for tea," the jukebox roared, "and me for you and you for me..."

"Ya get some salmon eggs, and ya take and dump 'em in a net, and ya hold the net unna water so the milk rises offen the salmon eggs..."

"Abraham Lincoln is right, Mrs. Nussbaum, and now can you name a second one, he was a famous Civil War general."

"...and ya let a coupla bullheads swim inna ya net, see, and then ya lift it quick..."

"Try and think now, Mrs. Nussbaum, his first name was Ulysses."

"...and ya take and thread ya hook through wunna the bullheads and ya hang the other one onna ya hook so it'll still wiggle, and ya let it way down inna the water, see." He gave me a wink, and drained his glass. "Ya'll catch a big one every time."

I thanked him, and bought him another drink and left. I wanted to get some sleep; tomorrow I would set out bright and early to find the deep run below the coffeepot boulder. I could find it again with my eyes shut. I would drive along an old lumber road as far as it would go, hike the rest of the way on foot, and climb down a steep bluff to the stream. No one ever got this far back; I was the only one who knew the secret pool.

Across the room the jukebox bellowed: "Nobody near us to see us or hear us..."

*E*ven the lumber road had been improved, I discovered. The brush had been cleared and the sides bulldozed to make it wider, and the surface was packed hard with constant travel. It seemed to go on end-lessly, but I noticed a side road to the right, heading in the general direc-tion of the stream. The tire ruts looked fresh as I turned onto it; other cars had used it recently. It terminated in a clearing on a high bluff, and I could hear the roar of the river below me as I climbed out of the car.

In front of me was a wooden sign with carved letters reading, "State Camp Site. Keep This Area Clean." Picnic tables and benches had been erected under the trees, and there were conveniently located metal waste-baskets to hold trash and a public latrine at one end of the clearing. Several trailers were parked at the edge of the bluff, and the occupants, in various stages of undress, were performing their morning ablutions. A small sign said "Coffee Pot Rapids" and pointed to steep trail leading down the side of the bluff. Steps had been cut here and there in the dirt, and there was a rustic handrail to make the descent easier.

The grass beside the stream was trampled, and I noticed some empty salmon-egg jars and a tangled length of monofilament line caught in a snag. I followed a well-worn path along the bank, and the river made a bend to the right, and at the head of the pool was the boulder. The stream parted around it, and the main channel hugged the far bank. The run looked shallow, and somehow the whole pool had gotten smaller, the way an old person shrinks with age.

I put on a number sixteen Quill Gordon, and made a long cast across the stream. The fly brushed the grass and dropped onto the slick, and something struck it. He broke water as I lifted the rod, and for a moment I had a picture of Old Faithful hanging there in space, halted at the height of his leap. I could see the drops of water standing in the air, the blue heron motionless in mid-flight, the marmot still frozen on the bank.

I reeled in. A little trout skittered toward me on top of the water, and I slipped a wet hand around him and lifted him gently. He might have gone eight or ten inches; I didn't measure him. He had a hatchery pallor, and his breath smelled strongly of liver. I removed the fly from his upper lip and put him back, holding him upright in the water until he regained his strength. He did not dart away at once; he swam around my feet, reluctant to return to the stream. I knew how he felt.

I heard steps behind me. My brother angler of the night before was floundering up the path, his knee-length rubber boots dislodging an empty beer can that rolled into the stream with a clank.

"Catch anything?" he asked me.

"I caught a six-pound rainbow," I said.

He didn't believe me, of course. I think he was a little hurt because I was making fun of him. "Yeah? Where?"

"Right there," I told him, and pointed to my secret pool, "over by that far bank."

It didn't matter any more. There was no need to keep it secret, because no one else could find it but myself. It would always be safe in my mind, the way it used to be, and Old Faithful would be waiting for my fly. I could take him again whenever I closed my eyes.

– Seven –

Compleating Ye Angler

Corey and his sometime writing partner, Alastair MacBain, wrote together for a number of years during the 1930s and '40s; however, it is fairly obvious once you have a sense of their work together, that their professional writing careers were merely a cover for their professed fishing avocations. The deal was they would do the serious work first—you know, mosey on up to Alaska to some lake that never had been fished by a white man before, and on the plane they'd finally complete a film script that a studio had been screaming about for weeks. You see, as consummate fishermen, Corey and Mac always put their priorities first.

The following appeared in the South Bend Fishing Catalog of 1938. If nothing else, it shows how innovative a fisherman can be.

Each year, this South Bend outfit is making it harder and harder for fishermen. Each year they put out a bigger and better catalog, full of more tackle than you can shake at the end of a stick. Each year they bring out another hundred-page booklet with pictures of tempting plugs and luscious spinners and appetizing spoons and other delectable dinguses to satisfy the fishingest bug that ever dropped all his work to pore over its pages all spring. It's a wonder we fishermen ever get any business done at all.

The only trouble is that the catalog isn't complete. In vain we have searched through its pages for several items that every angler needs. It is in an effort to bring this booklet right up to the minute, therefore, that we submit a few more suggestions. We offer them free, for what they are worth:

I. **Angler's False Face**

Every fisherman knows that the first principle in angling is to fool the fish. Never let him know what you are up to. Catch him off his guard.

For this purpose, we offer our up-to-date Fisherman's Disguise, consisting of a complete set of beard and whiskers, a limp, a long, longitudinal scar across the left cheek, and the fictitious name of "Harry." This outfit is guaranteed to fool any fish completely, and as a result the unsuspecting trout or bass will "bite" at once before he realizes his ludicrous mistake.

This disguise is also useful for the angler to wear home at night in case he doesn't get any fish.

No. 886—False beard and whiskers (choice of colors) $0.50

No. 23—Dark blue spectacles, cane, and sign, "I am Blind" $0.49

II. **Non-Snarl Casting Line**

A snarling line is one of the most unpleasant things to have along on a fishing trip, as its incessant grumbling and complaining will often spoil an otherwise pleasant afternoon on a stream.

Our new South Bend "Non-Snarloreno" model avoids this difficulty by a very simple device: Each inch of the line is carefully numbered. In the event of a backlash at No. 26, for example, all that the angler needs to do is to start with the number where the tangle occurred and read backwards from No. 26 to 25 to 24, etc., thus eventually solving the snarl and reaching the beginning of the line just in time to reel it in and start back home before it gets too dark.

No. 131 (with luminous numbers) ....$35 per yd.

III. **The Bing-Oreno**

A distinct innovation in angling. No trouble landing the captive, no bother removing the hook, no need of even cleaning the fish. These life-like worms, filled with our finest grade nitroglycerine, are lowered to the fish, who swallows them ravenously. All the angler needs to do is to raise the fish to the surface, hit him over the head with a baseball bat, and as he descends, catch him in a bucket. Makes Sport a Pleasure!

No. 99 (with Babe Ruth baseball bat) ....$0.99 ea.

IV. **The All-Day Sucker**

No fisherman is complete without his pipe. It is his closest companion during the day. It is always clamped between his jaws when the "big one" is landed. Even if he forgets it then, you will invariably find it there that night when the photograph is taken.

As a result of such constant use, of course, the average pipe is apt to become a little waterlogged toward the cnd of the day, and often a good drag will produce a choking sound like the drain in the kitchen sink. To prevent this difficulty, we offer our special Self-Bailing Pipe for Fishermen. By means of a small hand pump attached to the bowl, the fisherman may keep it purring sweetly from morning to night without even removing the stem from his mouth.

No. 77 — The Scuppers (with rubber tubing) $4.98

V. **Retrieve-Oreno**

Here is the last word in educated plugs. Not only will this intelligent creation scent the fish and hold its point until the fisherman has time to find a good-sized rock to throw, but in addition it will swim out and get the fish, bring it back to shore, drop it at the feet of the triumphant angler, and stand wagging its tail eagerly and gazing up soulfully at its master with big, painted red eyes.

No, 23—"Rover" (with lead, harness, and whistle for field work)
....$1.00 per doz.

VI. **Lyfe-Lyke Rubber Fish**

Avoid the embarrassing features of an empty creel. Overcome your friends' tendency to smile and inquire, "What, no fish?" Do away with the necessity of stopping at the butcher store on your way home at night. Try our special Lyfe-Lyke Rubber Fish. These convincing little accessories are constructed like balloons, and when deflated may be carried conveniently in the hip pocket. At the end of the day they may be blown up to any size, depending on the angler's personal reputation as a fisherman, and swung casually from the left hand, or else held out in front of the camera.

No. 26 ....$2.50/doz.

Eight

It's the Secret of Success

This is one of those stories about a man named Binks. Only, as a matter of fact, his name is really Binks; and the fact that all those essays have been written about him in *Punch** doesn't seem to disturb his serene self-confidence in the least. I rather doubt if he is even aware of it.

Binks wanted me to go fishing. I am always ready to go fishing, under any conditions, and I didn't see how Binks would interfere with the fun. He had a gorgeous place he'd discovered—up in the Laurentides Park, north of Quebec—you never saw such fishing. Five-pound trout were nothing uncommon—one guy he knew caught three babies averaging that in the first hour—Lord! And easy to get to. Canadian National to Quebec; or—hold on!—we'd take his car. Make up a party of four. You had to have a permit from the Quebec Government, but he'd already attended to that. Gorgeous country; efficient camps and guides; best September fishing in the East.

For that matter, Binks was right about the fishing. The afternoon we arrived, I tried a number eight Montreal wet; and when I had hooked a four-pound speckled, I put on a dry Silver Doctor affair I had tied on a number ten hook and had the pleasure of seeing fly, leader, and all go sailing down below the dam in the wake of the biggest trout I'd ever established even a brief contact with. Binks elected to stay at the dam—he'd just turned over something pretty good—and I wandered downstream. My fishing partner met me later, on his way back, with a proud specimen dangling by its gills from his forefinger, and a blood-curdling story of a half-hour battle in swift water. So we ambled back to the dam and found that the fourth member of our party had taken three fair

---

Punch — the British humor magazine famous for its merciless caricatures

fish in the pool above the flume. Binks was still dropping his fly neatly over the nose of the trout he had spotted.

"Like the fishing here?" he grinned to me out of the corner of his mouth. A brown bump rippled the surface of the pool for an instant and he struck his fly too soon.

"Great!" I glowed, lighting my pipe and watching him. The black flies were around a little. "Never saw such water." My partner had gone up to Bink's car and stowed his rods in the rear; the other fellow had already climbed in and flopped on the cushions. "I want to work downstream from here tomorrow."

"Oops!" This last was occasioned by the fact that Binks had struck again too swiftly. A square, brown tail turned over once like a dolphin. Binks glanced over his shoulder at the line that had flopped back limply and lay tangled behind him in the bushes. "Do you mind?"

"Getting a bit dark," I suggested tentatively as I disengaged it for him. He stripped it in and cast farther out over the pool. "We're ready whenever you are, old man."

"Oh, this light will be good for an hour yet," said Binks easily.

I left him and joined the others at the car. My partner was anointing himself with fly grease and smoking vigorously. Our fourth was trying to sleep. He mumbled apologetically, "Couldn't sleep in that damned hotel last night."

"We'll take it easy tomorrow," I agreed.

It was after nine when Binks joined us at last. It seems he'd found a pool downstream and had on a fish that weighed—God knows how much it must have weighed. He wouldn't say. He lost the way twice while driving back to Taschereau, speculating about its weight, and it was something like ten before we had supper. "Plenty of time to unpack tomorrow," said my partner as we pulled off his boots.

"I'm going to get mine done tonight," said Binks briskly. "We want to get an early start."

I didn't pay much attention to that remark at the time. I was nearly asleep....

I thought I was being kicked by a horse that was climbing down the wall over my bed, and then I sat up and stared at Binks, with the chill that comes from being awakened too suddenly several hours before normal. Binks straightened over me in the dim grey light and smiled. "Four o'clock," he explained cheerfully. "We ought to be getting out on that stream."

"By God—I mean." I watched him lean over and thump my partner between the shoulders. "I mean, four o'clock, Binks?"

"It'll be five by the time we get going," said Binks. "We've only got a few days here. You don't want to miss the best fishing just because it's four o'clock," he explained.

It was not much after six that evening when we returned; but that was because we had fished downstream to camp, and our *hotelier* sent his son to tell us dinner *c'est se prepare*. Binks was happier when he realized he could get in a full evening's fishing afterward. The rest of us stowed our day's catch in the ice house; six fish, over twenty pounds. Binks hadn't any. That is, he'd had one great strike, but his leader was weak; and another one got off because the barb was broken on his fly. "Must have been six or seven pounds. I hear there are tremendous ones here in the lake, right near the camp. I know a guy who got one there once, weighed six pounds."

"I was thinking of a little poker after supper tonight," suggested my partner tentatively.

Binks tried to be tolerant about it. "Well, of course, if you're tired. But with fish like this...you can always play poker. I thought you were a real fisherman," he laughed, and winked to me.

We didn't get back from the lake until nearly ten, because after Binks had reeled in his line without a strike, my partner made one cast and hooked into a five-pounder that towed us all over the lake. As a result, next morning Binks let us sleep till half-past four; but we made up for it by missing supper altogether. It seems Binks had his first strike of the day on a light-colored fly, just at dusk—something tremendous, he said—and he had an idea that a White Miller floated downstream would do the trick. "You don't mind waiting, of course?"

My partner glanced at me. I nodded, and daubed on some more fly dope patiently; but there was a new look of determination in all our faces. When Binks returned a couple of hours later, empty-handed, he found us talking in low, guarded tones.

The following morning Binks sounded reveille at four. I sat up almost too abruptly in bed and faced him with a disarming smile.

"Listen, old man," I suggested, "that stream is pretty small for four men. Why don't you take it alone today?"

"Where will you fish?" he asked suspiciously.

"Oh, we thought we'd try the lake," I answered easily. "There's tremendous fish here in the lake, you know. Why, this friend of mine named..."

Binks got back early that evening; not much after seven. I saw him as he mounted the steps of the camp and stopped dead short in the doorway with a tragic expression on his face: disappointment, disillusionment, and outright rage. I suppose we *were* a rather slovenly outfit. Our boots were unlaced, our hair mussed; in fact, my partner was still wearing his pajamas. An empty bottle lay on its side in a corner, and another one stood nearly empty on the table. Our other companion was dealing cards

with some difficulty. The air was blue with smoke.

"How many fish did you get?" asked Binks in a strained voice.

My partner glanced at the guy dealing the cards and he, in turn, glanced at me. "We didn't get any," I replied slowly. "We didn't go out."

"You didn't go out," repeated Binks bitterly. "I bring you up here to the best fishing grounds I know, and you sit around all day—playing poker. I thought you were fishermen. How do you expect to catch anything if you don't go out?"

He paused and then held up a trout dramatically. It must have weighed every bit of three pounds.

"You got to stick at it every minute, like I do," said Binks.

– *Nine* –

Another Fisherman in the Family

> The reason this tender story reads so well is because it is absolutely true, and Corey observed it firsthand. He had no son, but he loved children and was sensitive to the glint of excitement in their eyes. That shines through in "Another Fisherman in the Family."

He could always tell when it was fishing time. His father would go upstairs right after dinner and he could hear him moving around the attic, looking for his wading boots and his canvas jacket with all the pockets and his old hat that smelled of fish. Sometimes he would come to the head of the stairs and shout, "What did you do with my red checkered shirt?" and his mother would call back, "It's right on the top shelf where you put it." Later, when he was supposed to be asleep, his father would tiptoe downstairs and get his aluminum rod case out of the hall closet and look his rod over carefully and maybe put it together in the living room and flick it once or twice, and all the time he would be humming a song to himself, sort of a funny song without any special tune, that the boy knew meant fishing. Then early the next morning, his father's partner would drive up in front of the house; they would hurry through breakfast, and then he and his mother would stand in the window and wave to them as they walked down the path together and got in the car and drove away.

He never could go along. His father would tell him, "Not yet, Bill," or, "You stay home and take care of your mother." Once, when his father and his father's partner were leaving on a trip, he packed his suitcase with a pair of rubber boots and a game called Fish Pond and his celluloid fish from the bathtub and followed them to the door, and they stopped and looked at each other and sort of grinned, and his father rumpled his hair and told him: "Maybe when you're a little older."

That didn't make any sense, of course, because he was four-and-a-half years old, going on five, and he knew a lot of things about fishing. He used to help his father tie trout flies, sitting on a stool beside him and not touching anything, and his father always let him hold the reel while he pulled off the line to grease it, and he even had his own fishing rod. Last Christmas, his father gave him a real rod made of all metal, with a reel you could actually wind and regular cuttyhunk line and hooks and sinkers, and he took it out of the case and put it together and flicked it around the living room, just the way his father did, until he broke two Christmas tree ornaments and knocked over a lamp, and his mother made him take it outside. "One fisherman in the family is bad enough," his mother said, looking at his father, who was hiding behind the newspaper.

He took the fishing rod with him that summer when they drove up to visit his father's partner in New Hampshire. There was a lake with some nice bass in it, the partner told his father, and every day the two of them would drive off together to fish the lake while he stayed home and took care of his mother, and every night they would come home again without any bass, and usually they had to pour a couple of drinks because they said they had such a bad day. He did not understand how you could have a bad day if you were fishing, but they seemed so unhappy that he drew a picture of a bass with his crayon set and gave it to them.

He wasn't quite sure what a bass looked like, but he used a lot of purple, because he liked purple, and he put yellow spots on it and drew a lot of jagged teeth, and his father's partner said it looked more like a bass than anything they'd seen in the lake that day. His father's partner was smoking a pipe, and he pulled on it for a while, and said: "Why don't we take Bill along tomorrow? Maybe he can show us what a bass is like."

"I guess we need somebody to show us," his father said, pouring himself another drink because he was so unhappy.

"Only be sure he doesn't fall out of the boat," his mother said, and his father grinned and said wasn't that just like a woman.

Tomorrow was like Christmas, it took so long coming. He woke up his father before it was light to ask him if it was tomorrow yet, and he was so excited he couldn't eat his breakfast. He took his fishing rod and reel and line and hooks and sinkers, and they walked down the path together to the car, he and his father and his father's partner and his mother, of course. She said she wasn't going to fish, but she wanted to watch from the bank in case he fell out of the boat, and he asked his father if that wasn't just like a woman, and his mother said something about little pitchers with big ears. They stopped behind the barn to dig some worms, and he didn't exactly like to touch them at first, but his mother said, "ugh," so he held one in his hand all the way down to the lake, just to show her he was like a man.

It took a long time to walk through the woods to the lake, because he had to stop every couple of steps to look at something new. His father and his father's partner kept telling him to hurry, but there were so many exciting things along the way. There was a squirrel's nest, and a lizard, and some pink moccasin-flowers, and a porcupine climbing a tree, and a pile of freshly chewed branches in the brook that his father's partner said was a beaver dam. His father's partner seemed a little surprised. "I've walked down this trail a thousand times," he said, "but it's the first time I ever noticed that dam."

He sat in the stern of the boat beside his father, while his father's partner took the oars and rowed out to a patch of lily pads, and dropped a stone for an anchor. His father threaded a worm on the hook, threw it over the side, and gave him the rod to hold. He held it in both hands and waited. His nose was just level with the gunwale of the boat, and in front of his eyes he could see a million tiny bugs running around on top of the water. His father couldn't see them because he was sitting too high. Sometimes the waves made the lily pads move up and down, and on one of them a bright green beetle was eating a hole in the leaf. He told his father about the beetle, but his father said, "Don't take your eyes off the rod."

It was hard to keep his eyes on the rod, because there were so many other things to see. A big, blue darning needle zigzagged across the lily pads, and a black and red turtle was sunning itself on a log, and a kingfisher flew out of a tree with a loud whirring sound and dipped over the water and flew back to the tree again. He heard a splash beyond the lily pads, and he saw something swimming along the shore, with just its nose out of water. He started to ask his father about it, but just then his father said, "You've got one on! Lift your rod!"

He lifted the rod with both hands, and the line felt heavy. His father said: "Reel it in." He turned the handle of the reel, but the line kept going farther and farther out, and his father said: "No, turn it the other way." He reeled the other way as fast as he could while his father held the rod so he wouldn't drop it, and a fish came right up out of the water, and he kept reeling, and the fish followed the line all the way to the tip of the rod, and his father said, "That's enough," and he lowered it into the boat.

His father took the fish off the hook and tossed it in the bottom of the boat at his feet. It was the most beautiful thing he had ever seen in his life, all purple and orange and blue, like the colors in his crayon set. It flared once or twice, splashing water onto his sneakers, and in the sun all the different colors looked like a lighted Christmas tree. His father's partner shook his head and said: "You know, I never realized before how pretty a sunfish could be."

While his father was baiting the hook again, his father's partner put on a pair of dark glasses, the kind you can see under water with, and looked down over the side. Suddenly he said in a low voice: "Good gosh, do you see what I see? Sit still." They all sat still, and after a minute his father's partner said: "That was at least a three- or four-pound bass. I saw him turn once, and then he ducked under the lily pads. Get the line out there quick." His father's hand was trembling as he finished putting on the worm. He pulled off a lot of line from the tin reel, and looped it in his hand, and tossed the worm out to the very edge of the pads. It

Corey Ford Archives, courtesy of Dartmouth College.

landed with a little plop! and sank, and the loops of line followed it until the line was straight down. His father gave him the rod again and whispered: "Hold it tight in case he strikes."

He waited, but nothing happened. Everything was very still. The lily pads moved up and down with the waves, and perfectly round drops of water balanced on the leaves like loose pearls. The tiny little bugs still scampered back and forth beside the boat, and the kingfisher flew down out of the tree again, and he saw the blue darning needle dart across the water toward him. It hovered in the air for a moment, without moving, and then it lit on his wrist.

His father's partner was peering down into the water with his dark glasses. "I think I saw him turn again," he murmured. "Right behind the bait."

He was staring at the darning needle. He could feel the legs prickle his skin, but he didn't move his hand. Its four spotted wings were thinner than tissue-paper, so thin you could almost see through them, and its long, beautiful blue body shone like a mirror. Its legs were right up behind its eyes, and the eyes were bigger than its whole head, as big as blueberries, and they seemed to be able to see everywhere at once. The end of the body dipped and straightened again, and he held his breath.

His father's partner said: "He's got it! He's on!" and his father shouted: "Lift the rod!"

But if he lifted the rod, he'd move his hand, and that would scare the dragonfly. It was still poised on his wrist, its tissue-paper wings motionless, its eyes seeing everything. Then his father reached for the rod, and the dragonfly darted away so quickly that he never saw it go, and he lifted the rod, but it was too late. The bass was gone.

His mother was waiting on the bank as he jumped out of the boat and ran toward her, carrying the string of sunfish on a forked stick. He was so excited he could hardly talk. He told her about the kingfisher, and the tiny little insects running around on the water, and the green beetle, and the drops of water on the lily pads, and, oh yes, the turtle, and the thing he saw swimming along the shore, and the bright blue darning needle that lit for a minute on his wrist. The words tumbled over each other, because there was so much to tell her.

His father's partner whispered, "He doesn't seem very disappointed about the bass," and his father said, "I guess he's forgotten it."

He hadn't forgotten about the bass, but it didn't make a difference, because there were so many other things. That's what fishing was. That was something he would have to show his father and his father's partner, but, of course, there would be plenty of time to show them, because from now on they'd be fishing together all the rest of their lives.

He held up the string of sunfish, and his father's partner took a picture of him, and his mother said: "Now we've got another fisherman in the family." She was so proud, laughing and, at the same time, almost crying, that he and his father and his father's partner had to grin at each other, because wasn't that just like a woman?

Ten

How to Live with a Fisherman

My uncle lived for fishing. It was his favorite sport during fishing season, just like hunting was his favorite sport during hunting season. And when it was neither season, he'd be on the golf course only as long as there was daylight. He and my aunt lived in a fashionable apartment in New York, and about a month before opening day, the chintz sofa would be littered with rods, the dining room table cluttered with tackle, and, instead of nylons hanging from the shower rod, Unc's waders would be there.

My aunt, during the times when her husband was either absent or incommunicado, kept herself busy, for she too was an inveterate sportswoman. During fishing season she would fish for sales at Bloomingdales; during hunting season she would hunt for bargains at Saks; and when she was a golf widow, she'd sink one heck of a hole in their joint checking account while jogging up and down Madison Avenue. For she had perfected the art of "How to Live with a Fisherman."

Statistics show that more than sixty million Americans go fishing every year. But what about all the other millions who have to put up with them? I mean the long-suffering people that the people who fish are married to.

Consider the wife of an ardent angler. All her husband talks about is fish, fish, fish. He dreams of fish. He even smells slightly of fish. His necktie is embroidered with trout flies, and his tie clasp is a miniature rod and reel. His highball glasses are decorated with leaping rainbows or bass. The framed still-life over the mantle, which his wife painted in art class, has been replaced by a stuffed tarpon. Instead of carrying his children's pictures in his wallet, he has a snapshot of the twenty-pound striper he caught off the Cape last summer.

All season long her home is a shambles. The front hall is littered with discarded rods and creel and net. His wading brogues leave wet prints on the living room carpet, his sopping trousers are hung across the fire screen to dry, he drapes his socks over the dining room radiator. If he cleans the day's catch in the kitchen, he leaves her dishpan full of severed fins and heads, and fish scales are stuck to the linoleum floor for her to skid on. If he cleans them in the garage, they attract the neighborhood cats. Nobody can use the bathtub, because his waders are dangling inside-out from the shower curtain rod. He dumps his live minnows in the tropical fish aquarium every night so they'll keep nice and fresh. The other day, I read about a worm fisherman's wife who sued for divorce because he parked his night crawlers in her pot of African violets and then forgot to tell her.

The worst of it is that fishing fever is a year-round disease. A golfer's wife has a chance to get acquainted with her husband once the snow comes, but the angler's wife is lucky if he recognizes her when they pass on the street. During the winter months, he sorts over his tackle or buries himself in a fishing catalog, nodding vaguely and murmuring "Hmmm?" when she tries to make conversation. His eyes grow glazed as spring approaches. On opening day, he leaves the house before dawn and doesn't show up again till dark. His wife can't go anywhere because he has the car. He comes home with a severe head cold—the only thing he caught all day—and goes to bed right after supper so he can get an early start the next morning. If his neglected spouse packs her suitcase and flounces home to mother, it may be several days before he notices that she's gone.

Such marital spats may be avoided if the wife displays a little tolerance for her helpmate's foibles. Many a happy home has broken up merely because the husband takes his summer vacation in Canada with the boys, or arrives home two hours late for dinner and then keeps it waiting another hour while he invites his fishing cronies in for just a quick one. All these minor differences can be resolved if the angler's wife will follow a half-dozen simple rules:

Rule One. When talking to a fisherman, learn to employ the right terms. A dry fly purist will wince perceptibly if you call his split bamboo rod a "pole," or his enameled tapered line a "string." It is equally important to know the proper remarks to make. When he returns empty-handed after a luckless afternoon, for example, never ask: "How many did you get?" If he holds up one very small trout, don't say: "Isn't it cute?" Bolster his ego by exclaiming, "Wait a minute, dear, till I get the camera."

Rule Two. Don't fly off the handle when he filches your manicure scissors or a spool of silk thread off your dresser. Avid fly tiers keep their eyes peeled for any useful material and are unable to resist plucking a couple of tail feathers from the parakeet, or unraveling some wool from the baby's sweater, or snipping a few strands from your chinchilla coat. Grit your teeth and smile sweetly as he empties the pill bottles in the family medicine cabinet for something to keep his flies in, or cuts out the palm of your rubber kitchen glove to patch his waders.

Rule Three. Never (repeat, never) touch his fishing tackle. Every fisherman is convinced that someone has been tampering with his equipment and will shout downstairs accusingly to his wife: "What did you do with my sunglasses?" or, "Where did you deliberately hide the suspenders for my waders?" and there's no use aggravating his phobia further. Take the wife of a fisherman I know who decided to clean up the mess in his tackle room while he was away. She emptied all the contents of his aluminum fly boxes into one pasteboard carton labeled "bait." She removed his trout lines from their respective reels and wound them up together like a ball of yarn. She took everything out of the pockets of his canvas jacket and sent it to the cleaners and gave his battered fishing hat to the church rummage sale. It cost him five dollars to buy it back, and he left home for a month of salmon fishing and grew a beard. What's more, he refused to shave it off until she promised never to set foot in his tackle room again.

Rule Four. If his fishing partner is planning to pick him up at five a.m., the understanding wife will set her alarm for four in order to wake him, get his breakfast ready, and make some sandwiches for his lunch. Usually he will go back to sleep again until the partner honks his horn in the driveway. He finishes pulling on his boots as he dashes downstairs, shouts over his shoulder that there's no time for breakfast, and bolts out the front door. Don't be upset if you discover the sandwiches still on the hall table an hour later. It will save your making lunch for him tomorrow.

Rule Five. Encourage him to tell you about the big one that got away. Don't let on that you've heard the same story a thousand times before, or interrupt to remind him that the fish has gained a little more weight with each telling. If you have guests for the evening, ask him to show the color slides of his canoe trip to Maine. Not only will your husband be delighted, but you'll get rid of the company early.

Rule Six. Last but not least, don't try to share his hobby and accompany him on a fishing trip. You'll spend your whole day running back up the trail to fetch his landing net or climbing a hemlock to disengage the fly he hung up on a backcast. Not only that, but you'll have to listen all the way home while he explains that the water was too high or too low; it was too hot or too cold; the wind was too windy; or you got in his way while he was casting.

If you do go along with him and happen to hook a larger one than he does, remove the barb when he isn't looking and let your trophy swim away. It's better to lose a fish than a husband.

A final suggestion: Never ask a fisherman why he goes fishing, because he can't tell you. How can he make you understand that it's more than the fish he takes? It's the sound of running water, the smell of damp rocks, the slap of a beaver's tail or a fawn standing beside the stream at dusk. It's all the memories that crowd in on him of other fishing trips, of campfires that he squatted beside, of friends he used to know. So if he comes home at night with his nose running and a blister on his heel and one eye swollen shut where a black fly nailed him, don't waste your sympathy on him. Feel sorry for yourself.

You married a fisherman.

Eleven

Trout Widows

The papers were filled with the details of the Twitchell's divorce last week. You may have noticed it, because it was rather an unusual case. All the wife did, according to the story, was to send her husband's felt hat to the cleaners. "Absolutely all I did, Your Honor," she explained to the judge, in filing suit on the grounds of desertion, incompatibility, and cruel and unusual punishment, "was to take this dirty old hat that he'd been wearing for years, with grease stains all over it and the top crushed in like a muffin and the hatband practically ripped to pieces where he'd kept trout flies in it, and send it around the corner to be cleaned and blocked. And then he came home, took one look at it, and began smashing the furniture, and setting fire to the house in several places."

I knew the husband in this case pretty well, as it happened. His name was Herbert Twitchell, and he was as mild-mannered and considerate a chap as you would ever want to go fishing with. He belonged to the Mayfly Club on the Beaverkill, and he was one of the most popular anglers on the stream. I never saw him lose his temper when his backcast caught on a balsam, or a heavy shower came up just in time to spoil the evening hatch, or when he got pebbles down inside his waders. We all thought a lot of Herbert, but I must admit none of us was particularly surprised when things sort of blew up with him at home. We had seen it coming for a long time.

"In fact, I wouldn't be surprised if it happened any day now," Mac was saying at the Mayfly Club only the other evening. We had all dropped into Charlie's room as usual after we had come off the stream, to have a quick one and hear Charlie tell how the barb came out just as he had his trout at the net or it would have gone easily three pounds, maybe four or five, and the conversation drifted around to Herbert. "I mean, he hasn't shown up here at the club for several days," Mac said, leaning back in

Charlie's chair and crossing his boots on Charlie's pillow, "and you take the way he's been acting so funny lately and all, I personally wouldn't be at all surprised if she—" He paused just a moment on the word "she"—"had been getting at him again."

"She's going to get at him once too often," Cliff nodded darkly, pouring himself another drink from Charlie's bottle. "You mark my words."

"When a nice quiet fellow like Herbert lets go," said Tom, "he lets go all of a sudden. Like a one-horse sleigh."

"Shay," slurred Charlie.

We all paused and looked at him expectantly.

"What is it, Charlie?" asked Tom.

"I just said 'shay,'" said Charlie sullenly. "Herbert's like a one-horse shay."

"That's just what I was saying," said Tom. "She's got him to a point where sooner or later he's bound to let go."

"You'd think a wife would more or less encourage her husband if he had some healthy outdoor hobby like fishing," said Mac, borrowing one of Charlie's cigarettes. "I mean, you'd expect that a wife would make some effort to share her husband's interests a little. Like, take my own wife, the other day she actually objected to cleaning some fish I brought home. She said she was sick of the smell of fish."

"I know how it is," Tom nodded. "My wife objects like that sometimes to my fishing coat."

"Speaking of fish," Charlie began eagerly, "I had hold of one today..." He trailed off.

We all looked at Charlie for a moment, and looked away again.

"Anyway," said Mac after a pause, "I wouldn't be at all surprised if something happened with Herbert almost any time. You can drive a man just so far."

"He's bound to crack sooner or later," said Tom.

Cliff nodded. "You mark my words," he said solemnly.

I guess that Herbert was pretty much on my mind, because I remember mentioning him to Mary when I got home from the Beaverkill that night. Mary is my wife and she really is what you might call the fisherman's ideal wife. That is, she never asks me whether my feet are wet; she never questions my alibis; she never objects if I borrow several choice feathers from her hat to tie some special pattern of fly, and in all the years that we have been married she has never asked me whether I wouldn't catch more fish if I used a worm. Other wives, like Herbert's wife for instance, are forever nagging their husbands and complaining about minor details like getting up at four in the morning to fix him a light lunch. Mary displays a sympathetic attitude toward my fishing, and she has never, so far as I know, exhibited the slightest symptoms of malignant anglerphobia, or an acute dislike for trout, which bothers so many women who marry fishermen. That is, up to the night I happened to mention Herbert.

As a matter of fact, the subject of Herbert arose in a rather curious manner. I was having a late supper. I know some men's wives get pretty wrought up when their husbands are late for supper and will fold their arms and tread around and around the kitchen with little puffs of smoke rising from the soles of their feet, but Mary always has everything piping hot, serves it without a word of complaint, and then sits and watches me eat it with a sad, sweet smile. Sometimes she murmurs, "I know those popovers are ruined, John; you don't have to pretend to eat them," or "I worked on that pudding for you all afternoon, but of course it's all dried out now after being in the oven three hours," and occasionally she will borrow my handkerchief to dab at her eyes a little—I have never understood why women who cry never carry their own handkerchiefs—but all I have to do is to pat her hand and tell her to go buy herself another bureau. Mary is very fond of antique furniture, and I can always fix things by telling her to buy another old chair or bureau. In the course of the past ten years, I have probably bought enough chairs and bureaus to furnish a sizable hotel. As I was saying, I was enjoying my supper and regaling her between mouthfuls with various items of news that I thought would be of interest.

"Like, for instance, you take a day like today," I told her, "all lowery and overcast. The average person would say under those conditions that a bright fly like a Coachman or even a Pink Lady would be the killer, but here were Tom and Mac and the others trying everything they had, and I put on this number fourteen Whirling Dun that I'd tied with medium-light starling wings, molefur body with two turns of gold tinsel around the hook at the end, glossy ginger-hackle legs, and just three whisks of it for the tail..."

I noticed that Mary was sitting in her usual attitude of rapt attention, with both elbows on the table, fingers laced together like a hammock, and her chin resting on her fingers. She kept nodding silently, "Of course," and her eyes wandered over the table, around the room, and up to the ceiling. I took another mouthful.

"Because you can say all you want about color," I insisted, gesturing emphatically with my fork, "but I personally think that trout must be aware of color, because otherwise how would they have distinguished my dark fly today and not paid any attention to Mac's or Tom's? It is my own personal theory..."

"John," said Mary suddenly, "do you like that stuffed trout over the mantel?"

I paused and looked at her in surprise. "Of course I like it," I said. "That's the first big rainbow I ever took out of the Beaverkill. In fact, that trout is really an illustration of what I was saying just now about color." I resumed eating again. "I remember I just happened to have a few Royal Coachmen that I had bought in a little tackle store near Roscoe that morning..."

I had a sudden cold premonition, and I set down my fork abruptly. "Mary."

"What is it, dear?"

"Mary," I said slowly, "why did you ask me just now whether I liked that stuffed trout?"

"I just wondered whether you like it, that's all."

"Did you think maybe I wouldn't like it? Don't you like it?"

"Of course I like it, dear, only I wondered whether it might look all right somewhere else."

"What's made you think maybe I wouldn't like it? Don't you like it?"

"Of course I like it, dear, only I wondered whether it might look all right somewhere other than over the mantel."

"What's the matter with it over the mantel? What else would you put over the mantel if you didn't have that trout?"

"Well," said Mary. "I thought maybe father's picture."

"Do you mean to imply," I almost shouted, "that you think your father is better looking than a stuffed trout?"

Mary began to cry. "My father was a fisherman, too," she said, a little irrelevantly, I thought.

"We won't say anything more about it," I said firmly, and I continued to eat for several moments in silence. "That trout will remain over the mantel, of course." I took another mouthful. "I hope I don't have to mention it again."

Mary shook her head.

"We'll just drop the entire subject, Mary, if you don't mind."

"Yes, John," she said.

"I prefer not to discuss it further."

"No, dear."

I put down my fork again. Another thought had just struck.

"As a matter of fact," I said, "how did you ever happen to think of moving that trout in the first place?"

"I don't know," said Mary. "I just thought of it."

"I mean, did anybody suggest it to you?"

She shook her head.

"Was your mother here today, by any chance?"

"No, John," she said.

"You mean to say you just thought of it by yourself?"

She nodded but didn't say anything.

I could feel a cold lump in the pit of my stomach.

"Mary," I said very slowly, "are you getting like that, too?"

"Like what, too?" she asked, a little frightened.

"Like Herbert's wife."

"Who's Herbert?"

"Mary," I said, "I think we ought to understand each other very plainly about this whole thing."

"Eat your supper, dear," said Mary.

"Mary," I said, "I don't suppose you know what this sort of thing could lead to?"

"Dear, please eat your supper."

"I don't suppose you realize that it's just this sort of thing that has practically wrecked the Twitchells' home. I don't suppose you are aware how little things like this have turned the Twitchells' life into a veritable living hell?"

"Who are the Twitchells?" asked Mary.

So I told her about the Twitchells...

The whole trouble with the Twitchells—as I tried to explain to Mary—was that Herbert's wife did not understand fishermen.

Herbert was a typical fisherman. That is, he had certain little traits and foibles that doubtless endear fishermen to their associates, but are apt to set them more or less apart from together people, such as their wives. These traits date back to prehistoric days when men used to live together in crude fishing camps and wring out their socks every night in the fireplace, and there is nothing whatsoever that can be done about them.

Fishermen, for example, always throw matches on the floor. No matter how many ashtrays their wives set in front of them, their matches always end up on the floor. They track their muddy boots through the house, and when they take them off, they scatter sand and pieces of sharp gravel on the rug beside the bed. They drop their waders on the front porch; they knot their wading shoes together and drape them over the bannisters; they take off their wet pants in the kitchen and they lay their underclothes to dry in the parlor. They use the best linen guest towels to wipe their reels. They leave fishhooks in upholstered chairs. They demand their breakfast at dawn— "Isn't that coffee ready yet? Here it is after four!"—and they are anywhere from two to six hours late for dinner. They are jumpy, irritable, and moody over the winter, and during late February and March, they are apt to break off abruptly in the midst of a conversation and sit staring into space for an hour. When they come home with a nice mess of trout they are insufferable, and when they come home without any fish at all they are unbearable. They always blame their wives for the weather.

Unfortunately, a wife who is married to a fisherman (and the same thing holds for golf-wives, hunting-wives, tennis-wives, bowling-wives, squash-wives, skeet-wives, badminton-wives, and the wives of those who sit all night and listen to the radio) never gets to see her husband often enough to learn to appreciate these tiny idiosyncrasies of his and make due allowance for them. An Antarctic explorer's wife, for example, sees her husband now and then between trips; even a flagpole-sitter's wife meets her husband while he is climbing down to change flagpoles. But a fisherman's wife only encounters her husband at odd moments, such as when he trips over her bed to turn off the alarm clock or bumps into her in the hall while carrying his tackle upstairs (for some reason, fishermen spend a great deal of time carrying their tackle upstairs and then carrying it downstairs again), and his remarks on these occasions are limited to comments like, "Where in the name of sweet gosh did you deliberately hide my socks with the red tops?"

The only thing that a wife can do under these circumstances is to take into account the fact that her husband is under considerable emotional strain and be careful not to heckle him with trifles such as household bills, the furnace, or the fact that his office phoned three times that day to find out where he had been. If a wife will make certain allowances for her husband like this and, in addition, keep out of his way as much as possible during fishing season, I said to Mary, she could avoid to a very large extent the trouble the Twitchells were having.

The Twitchells were married about two years ago, and everybody thought at the time that they would be very happy together. In fact, people referred to them as an ideal couple. "Herbert and Edith really make an ideal couple, don't you think?" they all said. Of course, Edith did not care anything about fishing, but Herbert assured us at the wedding reception that this was really a good thing. "For one thing, she'll never try to come along on a fishing trip," he laughed, putting his arm around her, "and fall out of the canoe, or get her hook caught in a tree, or throw back a trout because the poor thing seemed to be suffering." He kissed her. "Will you, honey?"

"I really don't know the first thing 'bout fishing," she confessed with a shy smile. "I wouldn't know one pole from another."

"Pole!" Herbert repeated, and nudged us with a wink. "She calls a rod a 'pole.' Gee, I get a kick out of that."

"I mean, I wouldn't even know how to work that little pulley that holds the string..."

"Pulley! String!" Herbert howled. "I ask you, isn't that cute?"

We all assured him that it was very, very cute.

They went to Florida for their honeymoon—Herbert had always had an ambition to try some of that tarpon fishing in the Gulf—and when they came back, they settled down in a comfortable little house in the suburbs. Herbert put all his fishing tackle in a special den of his own and never used the rest of the house except maybe to hang his rods in the kitchen while the varnish was drying, or to practice a little casting now and then in the parlor. They seemed to be very happy together. To be sure, he began to act more and more absent-minded as April drew near, and occasionally that faraway look would come into his eyes and he would begin to hum to himself or finger the pages of a fishing catalog idly. Once Edith asked him rather sharply: "Herbert, what on earth are you moping about?" But Herbert merely rose in silence, went upstairs to his den, and shut the door, and the incident was soon forgotten. The first sign of a rift appeared when Herbert showed up at the Mayfly Club that spring.

"How's Edith?" we asked.

"She's all right, I guess," said Herbert without much enthusiasm.

"Is anything the matter?"

"Well," said Herbert, "I kind of wish she wouldn't keep calling my rod a pole, that's all."

"I thought you said that was cute."

"It is cute," said Herbert, "But it sort of gets on your nerves after a while. Like when I come downstairs all dressed in my fishing clothes and carrying my waders and creel and rod case, I wish she wouldn't say: 'Are you going fishing?'"

"What's wrong with that?"

"Well, I suppose there's nothing exactly wrong with it," Herbert admitted, "but I wish she wouldn't ask me if I was sure I hadn't forgotten anything."

"She's probably just trying to be helpful."

"It's a little hard to explain," said Herbert. "But I wish at least she wouldn't tell me to be sure not to fall in and get wet. I guess I can fall in if I want to and get wet."

I looked at Mac, and Mac looked at me, but we didn't say anything.

As a matter of fact, the first serious breach did not occur until late that fall, long after fishing season was over. Of course, Edith did not clean up his den on purpose. She did not plan it out ahead of time and deliberately wait her chance until he went away. She just yielded to that impulse that most women have to rearrange things. She said later that all she meant to do was just to straighten up a few things here and there.

"I just happened to glance in the door and notice what a mess there was on the floor," she told her mother, when she was able to stop crying, "and I thought I'd try to fix it up for him as a little surprise. I thought he would be pleased."

Well, she got in there with her broom one morning, and she swept that floor as neat as a pin. She picked up a lot of stray flies, and old cleaning rags, and empty spools, and a leather glove with the fingers cut out, and some cigarette tins, and several odds and ends of silk thread, and she threw them all away. She took all his reels and put them in one drawer marked "Reels." She took his tapered lines off the driers and rolled them up into a neat ball and put them in a drawer marked "Lines." She took his rods out of their cases and wrapped them all together in a newspaper and put them on a shelf marked "Poles." She took all his flies and emptied them out of the various little aluminum boxes and celluloid boxes and pillboxes where he had kept them and put them all in one big pasteboard box marked "Flies." She put away his boots in the bottom of the closet, folded his shirts very carefully, and took everything out of the pocket of his fishing coat and hung it in the closet on a coat hanger. Last, but not least, she put a pink shade on the single bulb he had hanging over his workbench, spread a rug on the floor, and hung a pair of bright print curtains in the window.

Herbert came home, and went upstairs as usual to his den. Edith didn't say a word. She heard him open the door, and did not hear anything else for a while. She said he called her just once—"Edith!"—in the strangest voice, as though he were choking. She went upstairs, and there he was, standing stock-still in the center of his den, with perspiration on his forehead and his mouth opening and shutting slowly. Edith said the expression on his face was something she would never forget to her dying day.

He looked at her, then he looked at the room, and then he took the drawer marked "Reels," turned it upside down and emptied the contents on the floor. He took the drawer marked "Lines" and emptied it on top of the reels. He took the pasteboard box marked "Flies" and dumped all the flies on the floor on top of the heap. Edith said she was too frightened even to scream. He took all his rods and threw them on the floor, and added his fishing coat, and shirts, and boots, and his cleaning outfit, and his line greaser, and his rod varnish, and snippers, and trout knife, and folding net and creel, and the pink lampshade, and the print curtains, and he began to stir them around and around with an empty rod case.

"This," he said to Edith in that same sort of choked voice, "is the way I like things. This is the way I know where they are instead of being put away somewhere. This is the way I always keep them."

He gathered up everything inside the rug, knotted the corners of the rug together over the end of the rod case, and slung the whole thing over his shoulder.

"I am now going away," he announced to Edith. "I am going fishing in Jasper Park, and hunting in British Columbia and Alaska, and I am going to stay in the bush three months and sleep in my underwear and grow a mustache. And when I come back, I am going to have a look at this room, and if I find you have touched a single solitary thing, I am going back into the bush again. I trust that I have made myself clear."

He didn't actually go away for three whole months, because Edith got hysterical and asked some of us to plead with him, and she promised, on her word of honor, never to tidy up his den again; but he did grow the mustache, and he wears it to this day. He told Edith it would serve to remind her now and then that he meant what he said.

From that time on, Herbert was really a changed man. Slowly but surely he began to revert to type. When he was first married to Edith, he always spruced up and combed his hair and put on a coat for dinner, but as the breach between them widened and his domestic instincts began to yield to the old atavistic urge to hunt and fish once more, we noticed that Herbert seemed to slip back into his earlier habits again. He seldom shaved, would go without a haircut for weeks, and often came to dinner with his boots unlaced and his shirt open at the neck. He picked his chop bones up in his fingers, and several times we saw him wiping his hands on his pants leg. He took up drinking again, and singing ribald songs—Herbert always carried an effective tenor—and he would play poker all night as long as someone was willing to stay up with him. He spent more and more of his time at the Mayfly Club that spring, and we all observed that his visits home were growing shorter and shorter. His manner was becoming more savage, too.

"She objected to my fishing pipe today," he announced one night when he returned to the Mayfly after a brief visit with his wife. He always referred to his wife as "she" these days.

"Now, Herbert," we said, "you don't want to let a little thing get you."

"A little thing!" Herbert exploded. "I've had that pipe for fifteen years. I've smoked it in fair weather and in foul. I've bitten through the stem, and patched the bowl with adhesive tape, and soaked it in rum to freshen it now and then, and I love that pipe like I love my own—" He broke off short. "When she has traveled as far with me as that pipe has, and remained as sweet, then maybe she can have a right to object. That's what I told her today."

We lowered our eyes. I guess we all could see it coming by this time.

I shall never forget the day that Herbert arrived at the Mayfly wearing a new shirt. It was a bright green shirt, and he was smiling steadily as he drove up to the Club and waved his hand to us on the porch.

"She threw out my old fishing shirt," he called out rather cheerfully. His voice had a high, hysterical quality, and his face was flushed.

"Never mind, Herbert," we tried to say casually, as though everything were all right. "You've still got the rest of your outfit."

Herbert shook his head triumphantly. "She gave away my fishing pants, too. She found that old pair of corduroy pants I always wear, with both knees gone and patches in the seat, and she gave them to the man that takes care of our furnace. She said they were a positive disgrace."

We shifted in our chairs uncomfortably.

"I'm giving her one more chance," said Herbert, yanking his old fishing hat down firmly over his ears. It was battered felt with grease stains all over it and the top crushed in like a muffin and the hatband bristled with snelled flies like a half-plucked chicken. "One more chance, that's all. If she touches another single thing—"

We watched him in silence as he got in his car again and drove on...

*M*ary looked at me for a moment as I finished the story.

"Is that all?"

I nodded.

"And you haven't seen Herbert since?" she asked.

"We haven't heard a thing," I said.

Mary rose thoughtfully, gathered up the supper dishes, and took them to the kitchen without a word.

It was just a week later, to the day, that I saw the story of the Twitchells' divorce in the papers. As I said, we had expected all along that it was coming, but it was pretty much of a shock just the same. We were very fond of Herbert, and I guess all of us had more or less secretly hoped that it would work itself out somehow. I know the thing knocked me pretty hard. After all, Herbert was a decent, well-meaning chap, and he might just as well have married an understanding wife like Mary. It made a man realize how lucky he was, I thought to myself, as I walked home that night with the paper under my arm and sat down at the table and began to eat my supper in silence. Mary was unusually sweet and attentive; she kept filling my plate and offering me things she knew I liked, and she insisted on getting my pipe and matches when I was through. She even came and sat on the arm of my chair and lit my pipe for me. "Something worrying you, honey?" she asked, fingering my bald spot.

I took a deep drag on my pipe. "You remember I was telling you about Herbert," I said.

I thought her face blanched when I said, "Herbert."

"I don't suppose you've seen the papers," I said, handing her the newspaper.

She grabbed the paper, and her hands trembled so hard that it rattled. Her face was deathly white. I thought it was strange that she should take Herbert's misfortune so hard. She set down the paper with a little cry. "Oh, John," she said.

What's the matter?" I asked, somewhat startled.

"Oh, John," she said again in a stricken voice.

I noticed she was looking past my shoulder toward the mantel. I turned around and stared blankly at the mantel. The stuffed trout was gone. Her father's picture was hanging in its place.

I didn't say anything. I just looked at her. I suppose it was the way I looked, because suddenly she sprang to her feet, pressed her knuckles against her mouth, screamed, "Don't you dare strike me!" and rushed out of the room. I heard her run upstairs and slam the door of her room and slide the bolt in the door.

I sat for a long time gazing thoughtfully at the picture over the mantel. It was really the first time I had ever taken a good look at Mary's father. He had a long sad face, lined with care, with haggard cheeks and deep-sunken eyes. His eyes were the eyes of a man who had suffered.

He seemed to be looking down at me now from the wall with a look of sympathy and understanding in his eyes.

After all, as Mary said, he had been a fisherman himself.

– Twelve –

Men Are Fish

It's the old, old story: Boy meets Girl. Boy loses Girl. Boy hooks Fish. Boy loses Fish. Girl gets Fish. Sure, you've heard it a hundred times before, but it never seems to lose that certain something, does it?

Yes, "Men Are Fish" is just another one of those torrid love stories—but with a twist. Corey writes two gals into this tale; one woman is a dark beauty, deft at whipping a line, whose waders would hug all the right curves if they weren't made of that cumbersome waterproof stuff. The other doesn't know a dry fly from a worm, but she's all Mom-and-apple-pie, the girl-next-door— your average blonde nightmare with eyes the color of the limpid pool she's fishing and legs that just don't quit. Quite a dilemma for our hero?

Read on to find out who really gets hooked...

She was into it solidly. Her rod was arched in a tense curve, the tip quivered and rose and was yanked downward again with successive short, vicious jerks that bent it almost double; the taut line knifed the water in hissing circles around the stern of the rowboat. Her arms trembled and her shoulders were bent with the steady strain. She took up a momentary slack in the line with her reel, and lost the brief advantage at once in a sudden headlong rush that bore the small boat helplessly across the bay in the wake of the fish. Bill could hear her shouting to the guide above the frantic screech of her reel: "Row, can't you? He's taking it out too fast..."

Bill grinned and rested his oars in their locks for a moment, watching with amusement as the old guide backed water desperately in pursuit. She had buried the butt of her rod in the pit of her stomach, bracing her arms and waiting for the flying handle of the reel to halt. There was no stopping that powerful run. The big tyee charged the center of the early morning fleet like a maddened bull, scattering the other boats to the right and left as it towed its captor stern-first across the fishing grounds toward the weed-lined shore, back and forth across the treacherous bars, and out at last into the deep channel of Discovery Passage. The boat was a black speck upon the flat metallic surface of the bay, pearly grey and pink in the increasing dawn. Her voice rose distinctly over the water: "Look out, he's going under the boat! Do something, why don't you?"

Bill shook his head in admiration. "There's a battle," he sighed, grasping the oars again reluctantly and resuming his slow, monotonous progress back and forth across the bay. "She knows how to handle a fish."

The tiny figure in the stern of the boat shivered without replying. She crouched, hunched against the cold inside a man's oversized hunting coat, her legs in thin, blue dungarees coiled under her in the cramped space beneath the seat, her red, chapped hands holding the trolling rod dogged-ly behind the boat at the proper angle. Her eyes were glued to the tip that nodded steadily with each turn of the swivel spoon underwater. Bill stole another glance over his shoulder.

"I think she's bringing it in. Look, Janet!" He rested the oars and gazed excitedly. "Yep, the old boy's getting his gaff—"

"Bill!" said Janet suddenly.

He asked without turning: "What happened?"

"Strike," she said quietly. "Just as you stopped the boat. It's off now."

In the distance, against the glare of the morning sun, he could make out the silhouette of the guide rising in the boat, his gaff poised in readi-ness. The girl's voice rose: "Look out!" and then the guide made a sin-gle swift lunge at the water, reached over the side, and hauled a limp black shape across the gunwales. It landed on the flooring of the boat with a muffled thud that echoed across the bay. Already several other boats were making for the official scales of the Tyee Club, located on the narrow strip of gravel beach at the mouth of the Campbell River. Bill picked up the oars eagerly.

"Let's head in and find out how much it goes. I'll row you again after breakfast," he added carelessly.

He beached the rowboat hurriedly, stowed the oars under the seat, and bounded over the lapping water onto the smooth, dark sand. Janet lifted her trolling rod from the boat, jumped ashore alone, and followed his rapid stride up the boulder-strewn slope of beach. Before them the white-washed pole and horizontal arm of the Tyee Club scales towered starkly, like a miniature gibbet, and beyond the craning necks of the admiring anglers they could see a dark, oval form dangling inert from the notched metal bar. The group was inspecting the salmon in patent awe.

"Just forty-three pounds!"

"That's a silver button, of course."

"But I really don't deserve any credit," said the girl's voice, somewhere in the crowd. It was a low-pitched, resonant voice, and Bill noticed that it was curiously distinct among the other voices in the crowd. "It was all Mr. Siddon's spoon, wasn't it, Professor? I owe it all to his lucky spoon," she laughed. Her laugh was husky and a little mocking. "Professor, may I have a picture of your lucky spoon?"

Bill halted at the edge of the group and stared enviously at the limp monster on the scales. The big tyee hung upside-down, suspended by a piece of baling wire that had been fastened around the base of its black, spade-like tail. Its fins were battered and frayed, its silvery sides streaked with sand and slime, and there was a red gash in its shoulder where the gaff had entered, but it had a real majesty about it still, a look of latent power, an expression of cunning in those tiny, pig-like eyes near the tip of its pointed snout. Its great mouth gaped loosely, and a concave silver spoon with a single red bead dangled from a loop of gristle in its jaw. Bill stooped and gazed curiously at the absurd slingshot that had felled this proud Goliath. Lucky spoon, eh? It had to be.

"—because I want one with the Professor in it," the girl's voice was saying. "You wouldn't mind snapping it, would you?"

"Billy," said Janet, jiggling his elbow.

"What?" said Bill absently. "Oh, sure." He rose with an apologetic smile. "I didn't realize you were—," then he met her eyes, and suddenly he gulped and looked down again in confusion. "Sure thing," he said gruffly.

She was smiling steadily as he found her image at last in the mirror of the camera. He stared at the miniature of her for a moment and tried to steady his hand. The diminishing effect of the camera's view-finder made her seem at once intimate and provokingly unattainable, as though he were peeking at her through a keyhole. The little image posed beside the salmon was even more beautiful than his first shocked impression had warned him. Here in the privacy of the camera's eye, he could study her frankly, at his leisure; his eye rose slowly in unabashed appreciation from her trim leather boots to the bold flare of her whip-cord breeches, to the snug knitted jacket that revealed the young curves of her body, the brown worsted cap crammed carelessly on her brown-red hair, the provocative smile upon her lips. The smile of the image in the finder seemed to be broadening, and suddenly he heard her husky laugh, very real and mocking, in front of him.

He raised his eyes in confusion, and felt the blood rush into his cheeks. "I'm sorry," he said, and released the shutter guiltily. His ears burned as he handed back the camera.

"Thank you," she said. She held out her hand. "I'm Lila Barett. The one on the right in the picture. The one on the left," she introduced gaily, "is Professor Siddon. He's really very distinguished," she smiled at the guide. "A student of psychology. Looks a little like Andrew Mellon, don't you think?" The old guide gazed at her stolidly. "The one in the center is the fish."

Bill grinned. "I'm Bill Walker."

"You don't need to tell me that," said Lila. "I followed you all four years you rowed for California. I saw you stroke that race against Washington last June—" She paused, and her gaze wandered significantly to the silent figure standing beside him.

Bill remembered Janet, finally. "This is Miss Evans," he introduced tardily. "I'm teaching her to fish."

Lila said, "Oh?" with an almost imperceptible rise of inflection in her voice. A single, expert glance out of the corner of her eye had appraised accurately the demure figure in dungarees and hunting coat. "You picked a good man to row you," said Lila, and dismissed her casually as she gestured toward the salmon. "But what shall I do with him? He's so noble, I couldn't eat him. It would be like eating my own grandfather. I wish I could have him mounted."

"It's easy enough," said Bill. "There's a good taxidermist in Victoria. You could probably ship him down on the noon train."

Lila looked helpless. "I don't know the first thing," she begged. "And I'd hate to have anything go wrong."

"I'll be glad to drive down to the station with you and arrange it," Bill began, and then remembered Janet again. "But I'd sort of promised Miss Evans—"

"That doesn't matter," said Janet in an unnatural voice. "Go right ahead. I'll wait here. Don't mind me."

A look of weary impatience crossed Bill's face. "Are you sure, dear?" he asked perfunctorily.

"I've got a little headache," said Janet dully. "I don't feel like fishing anyway."

She watched in silence as he shrugged and followed Lila toward the car. He moved with an easy slouching stride, his big body in a crew sweater and flapping whites dwarfing the slim girl beside him, his shoulders bent toward her attentively. His hand found Lila's arm as they moved together past the clubhouse. Janet turned away, her lips compressed. The Professor touched his hat.

"If you'd care to try for coho down by the inlet this morning, Miss Evans," he offered politely, "I should be free to row you."

"Thank you," she said wearily, "I'll wait here for Mr. Walker."

The Professor followed her eyes, and stroked his grey moustache thoughtfully. "Of course, it's really none of my affair," he began, "but if you'll forgive an old man for being personal, Miss Evans, perhaps I might suggest a bit of simple psychology—"

"As you said," Janet interrupted evenly. "It's really none of your affair."

"—about fishing," the Professor added mildly. There was a curious light in his deep, baggy eyes. "I thought I might show you one or two good things to know about fishing. There's a lot to learn about fishing..."

Janet nodded absently.

"Take the matter of playing a fish," the Professor began innocently. "So many people keep the line too taut. Whenever a fish feels a tight line, it will fight to get away. A fish hates to feel that it's hooked. The best-hooked fish in the world will try to break away if the line is too tight..."

Lila and Bill had reached the car. Janet took one or two indecisive steps forward. The door slammed, the starter whined, the car moved forward easily over the sand toward the road. Bill's arm was flung carelessly over the back of the seat behind Lila, and he did not look back. Janet hesitated uncertainly.

"Always give a fish its head when it starts to run," the Professor murmured. "That's the first thing to learn about fishing."

The car prowled over the crest of a hill and disappeared in a small spurt of dust.

"The coho should be working with the slack tide about ten," said the Professor gravely. "May I pick you up at Painter's Landing after breakfast?"

"I guess so," said Janet slowly.

He fingered his moustache for a moment as she trudged across the beach alone. The little muscles twitched suspiciously at the corners of his eyes as he stopped beside the salmon hanging from the scales, removed the lucky spoon carefully from its jaw, and held it aloft between thumb and forefinger. Solemnly, he took a chamois rag from his pocket and began to stroke the spoon, polishing its concave surface with a gentle soothing motion, as though he were caressing it, twirled the red bead and smoothed the twisted links of the swivel, wiping the metal bright and clean. He wrapped it in the cloth at last, and placed it carefully in his pocket.

The coho began to run just as the tide turned slack. A decent school had come in with the rising water that was already beginning to flood the exposed reefs and barriers of the inlet. They were feeding on the tiny herring fry that lurked in the kelp beds along the shore. As the salmon drove the herring up to the surface in frightened swarms, churning the water abruptly into a myriad of tiny geysers like a pelting rain, a flock of gulls wheeled overhead, screaming and diving headlong for them as they boiled helplessly on top of the water.

"You can spot your salmon by the gulls," said the Professor. "They always show you where the coho are feeding."

A dozen anglers in small boats were slowly rowing back and forth between the floating islands of kelp, their light bamboo fly rods poised in readiness, their eyes fixed on the gulls circling above the water. Over a wide, flat eddy near the shore, the birds hovered suspiciously for a moment, whirled, braked to a stop with a heavy flutter of wings, then plunged with shrill, triumphant screams. Simultaneously the flat surface of the eddy seemed to come all at once to a boil, countless little herring began to leap and dance in terror in the hissing water, and a big salmon rose in the midst of the swirl and smacked the water solidly in his descent.

The surrounding fishing boats closed rapidly, casting their flies over the spot. The eddy was a confused mulligan of salmon and fry and gulls and anglers, mixing together in a battle royal. A rod would bend with a sudden strike, a boat would detach itself from the group and follow its bolting captive across the bay, a reel howling gleefully in pursuit. Another angler would observe his fly mounting unaccountably into the air and circling over his head and curse vaguely at the sky as he leaned back and sought to reel in an irritable gull, fast to the end of his line. The herring bubbled frantically, the coho leapt and plunged, the gulls wheeled in screaming circles, several black ducks joined the free-for-all, diving and gulping the small fry underwater, while amid the fleet of small boats, an enterprising Japanese fish-merchant chugged complacently in his launch, tooted his horn above the din, and inquired amiably, "Any fish to sell? Any fish?"

"Try this fly, Miss Evans." The Professor knotted Janet's leader to a red-and-white streamer fly, tied on a long-shanked number four hook. "I dress them myself with polar bear hair. They have the shimmer of a little herring underwater."

Janet took the rod and cast dispiritedly into the swirl. The battle surging before her left her unmoved. Her eyes were dull, her mouth drooped, and now and then she glanced hopelessly across the bay toward the deserted channel, flat and simmering in the white heat of noon. Several gulls wheeled against the empty sky, and the smoke of a liner bound for Alaska smudged the distant horizon. For three hours she had scanned that horizon in vain for a sign of Bill. He'd had time to take Lila to the station and be back again a dozen times. He knew that Janet was waiting for him. She remembered Lila's graceful body in her tight knitted jacket reclining behind the wheel of the car, and Bill's arm hanging carelessly across the back of the seat behind her, and she smacked the fly clumsily onto the water with a vindictive flick of her rod.

"It's all in presenting the lure," the Professor cautioned her mildly. "You've got to make it look attractive to the fish. You can't force him to grab it, you know. You've got to tease him into wanting it..."

Janet lifted the fly irritably from the water, sent it back through the air and forward again, plunked it down once more into the center of the eddy. The sun was against her eyes; but in the middle distance, she thought she could detect a small speck on the horizon at last, heading toward them. Above the clamor of the gulls and splash of fish, she heard the faint *putt putt* of an outboard motor. The water boiled suddenly beside her fly, and a big salmon turned and plunged again.

"You had a rise," said the Professor. "Cast again a little to the left..."

The steady sound of the motor rose and fell vaguely over the water, now sharp, now muffled, increasingly distinct as it headed for the center of the channel. She could make out the little boat quite plainly now. Her eyes ached as she stared into the sun, trying to distinguish the occupants of the boat. She cast her fly impatiently over the nose of the salmon, and half-turned in her seat, shading her eyes. Bill's crew sweater was an unmistakable white blur in the stern of the boat; and then she recognized the diminutive figure beside him, her red-brown hair flung back, one arm braced behind her as she grasped the tiller. Janet caught her breath. Abruptly the rod was almost knocked from her hand, her reel chattered and began to screech as the salmon started his rush. She grabbed the rod and tried to check the fish.

"Play him!" the Professor shouted. "Give him his head. Let him run..."

The coho was taking out her line rapidly—a hundred feet, two hundred. The spindle of the reel grew dangerously thin. Her rod dipped almost to the water, wavered, and sprang upward again as the fish checked its run and leapt in a savage arc, its side flashing silver in the sunlight, its tail slapping the water with a star-shower of scattered spray. It hit, swirled, and charged forward again tirelessly. Above the whine of her reel, she heard the outboard motor putter once or twice, gasp, and suddenly cease. She stole a swift glance over her shoulder in time to see the little boat change its course, nose accurately between two points of rocks, and drift placidly out of sight into a sheltered cove along the shore. The rod shivered in her hands as the salmon leapt once more.

"Play him, Miss Evans!" the Professor urged. "Your line is too tight. Don't let him feel the hook..."

Her face was white with anger. She stared over her shoulder at the spot where Lila's boat had disappeared. In her mind she could see them sitting together in the stern of the boat, she could picture Lila's auburn head leaning back against Bill's shoulder, she envisioned her lips turned up provocatively. Janet's eyes snapped furiously. She began to reel in the salmon with quick determined fingers.

"Don't try to force him in! You can't make him come that way. Careful, Miss Evans," the Professor pleaded. "You're fighting him too hard. You'll lose him if you try to fight him. Let him run. There's time enough to lead him in later when he's tired himself out..."

She continued to turn the reel rapidly, horsing the fish toward her, her eyes fixed steadily on the point of rock that concealed Lila's boat. The coho came to the surface, saw the rod, lashed its tail, and kicked a shower of water behind it as it thrashed and plunged again. Her rod bent ominously. She scowled and worked the handle of the reel unheedingly. Once more the coho floundered to the surface, opened its mouth wearily, and rolled almost lazily over the line. She had a last glimpse of a silver shoulder turning underwater, the pink flash of her fly still in its jaw; and then her line went limp.

She continued to reel in the slack line stupidly for a moment. The slow tide had drifted them almost abreast of the cover, and she could see Lila's boat beached on the rocky point. Bill was standing knee-deep in the water beside the boat. As she watched, he lifted Lila lightly in his powerful arms and carried her, laughing, over the rocks toward shore, his whites flapping wetly about his legs, his soggy sneakers leaving black prints behind him as he climbed the sloping ledge. Janet looked away dully.

"Shall we go back to the camp?" the Professor inquired politely.

Janet looked at him thoughtfully for a long moment. Her eyes were hard and a little defiant. "I think I'd like to fish some more," she said at last. "There are still one or two things I need to know about fishing."

*T*he firelight played erratically over the rocks and bushes and the dark ceiling of pines overhead, and their rowboat was a black shadow on the beach at the water's edge. The tide *chunked* steadily along the thwarts of the boat, and the rising water lapped over the wet rocks at their feet and receded again, leaving little pools that glistened in the light of the fire. Janet sat with her knees drawn up under her chin, hugging her legs and gazing across the fire into the empty blackness of the bay, ominous and silent at night. The Professor poked the embers of the fire with a hemlock bough and laid it on the little blaze. It crackled upward cheerfully. Janet shivered. "Still cold?" asked the Professor.

"I'm fine now," she said. "It was a good idea warming up before we started back. It's dark, isn't it?"

The Professor kicked a half-charred log back into the fire. "I'm sorry," he apologized. "It's my fault we stayed so long. I've made you miss the night run of tyee down at Campbell River."

"I wonder if they'll worry about me?" Janet mused.

"I wonder," the Professor murmured mildly. He reached in his pocket and took out a small object wrapped in chamois. "By the way, Miss Evans, perhaps you would care to use this spoon on the tyee tomorrow? It's a spoon I've had for years. It's never failed me yet."

She took it curiously. "What's the red head for?"

"Just for luck," said the Professor. "It's not very important, but it helps to make the lure more attractive. Sometimes when a dark lure fails to attract a fish, it's wise to try a bit of color. That's another good thing to know about fishing. It's a lucky spoon."

"You believe in luck?" asked Janet idly.

"I believe in the spoon," said the Professor. "I suppose that's all that luck really amounts to. You've got to believe you're lucky. If you believe you are, usually you are. Calling a thing lucky sometimes helps. You need a little luck when you're fishing."

"I could use a little luck," said Janet, fingering the spoon thoughtfully.

"Luck," the Professor continued mildly, "and patience, and lots of backing on your line. That's the most important thing. You'll be all right if you have enough backing on your line."

Janet nodded. "Sometimes it scares you when the fish begins to run. Sometimes you think he'll never stop." Her voice trembled, and she gazed at the black water. "You wonder if he'll ever—come back. He just seems to be going farther and farther away—"

"That's when you need backing," said the Professor. "If you have enough backing, you'll be able to hold on until he's tired. You can sit back and wait while he runs himself out, and then you can lead him in so gently that he doesn't even know he's being led. You can lead him right up to your hand—"

In the distance the staccato *putt putt* of an outboard motor shattered the silence, drawing rapidly in the darkness. The Professor took out his pipe and knocked it on his heel.

"I think Mr. Walker is looking for you," he murmured innocently. "He's probably worried."

Janet gazed at him curiously across the fire. The fitful light made grotesque shadows in his sunken cheeks, and his beaked nose and long, sharp jaw were angular and unreal, like a face formed by the rocky ledges of a mountain. His face was very sober. She could not see his eyes. The sound of the motor grew louder as it headed up the channel toward them.

"Why do they call you Professor?" she asked quietly.

"Because I am a Professor," he said. "I taught psychology in a University once. I left because I thought it was better to practice than to preach..." He lit his pipe. "I'd rather fish," he said.

The motor thudded heavily toward them, and a lantern winked in the darkness over the water. She heard Bill's hail as he spotted the fire: "Janet! Is that you?"

"Here!" she replied, in a voice that was a little unsteady.

"You had us all half-crazy," Bill said angrily. He shut off the motor and headed the boat onshore. "I had no idea what could be keeping you so late. Lila let me borrow her motor to look for you," he explained, landing the boat and jumping onto the beach. "Are you all right?"

"Of course I am, Bill," she said pleasantly. "There was no need to worry. The Professor has been taking good care of me today. We've been working for coho. We just stopped a moment to warm up."

He glared at the Professor. "Maybe you don't know what time it is?"

"Time?" said Janet dreamily. "Dear, I've lost all track of time. The Professor was showing me some good things to know about fishing..."

"I suppose you didn't realize that maybe I'd worry," said Bill, in righteous self-pity.

"I'm sorry" said Janet contritely. "I thought you'd be trolling for tyee with Lila, you see. I never thought you'd worry about me."

Bill hesitated, and glanced uncertainly from her to the Professor. "We'd better be getting back," he announced at last. "The tyee will be running early tomorrow. We should be starting out about five to catch the tide—"

"Bill," she interrupted, "do you suppose Lila would mind awfully if we traded boats tomorrow? You could row her around, you see. I'm sure she'd let me have the Professor, just this once."

Bill stared at her. "Sure, I guess it would be okay with her."

"I want to try his spoon," Janet explained, gazing steadily at the Professor across the fire. "He's promised to let me use it tomorrow. It's a lucky spoon, you see..."

There are few moments of the day more dismal than that black hour just before the dawn. Janet shivered convulsively with nervousness and cold as she thrust her arms into the clammy sleeves of a canvas hunting coat and followed the Professor's lantern in the eerie darkness down the gravel walk from the cabin to the boat landing. Several figures were moving in the enveloping grey fog, and she heard a boat splash into the water and an oar scrape in the lock. The Professor steadied the rowboat against the pier and lifted his lantern as he helped her into the stern seat.

"All right?" he whispered.

She nodded in silence. Her face was pale in the uncertain light, but he noticed a spot of bright red under her throat. She fingered the scarf and met his inquiring gaze with a little smile. "Just for luck," she murmured.

She crouched in the stern as they shoved out into the black silence of Discovery Passage and moved cautiously over the bars into the deeper channel. Other shapes passed them in the weird half-light, members of the early morning fleet that were already trolling with the slack tide, and the rattle of metal oarlocks and steady splash of blades were ghostly in the hollow silence just before the dawn. The flat surface of the water was like a sheet of hammered pewter, and the sudden explosive leap of a young salmon beside the boat made her sit erect with a little gasp. The Professor rested his oars for a moment.

"You can start to let your line out now," he whispered.

He handed her the light tackle, regulated according to the Tyee Club specifications: a six-ounce bamboo rod, twenty-five pound test line, six-foot leader. For a moment he held the dangling spoon between thumb and forefinger, gave its gleaming sides a last affectionate pat with his chamois cloth, spun the red bead, and then flung it clear of the boat. She paid out the line slowly with her hand until she reached the white mark that indicated the Club's maximum trolling length of sixty feet. The swiveled spoon began to turn, the tip of the rod nodded steadily, the boat moved forward again.

"Watch the tip," the Professor cautioned. "You'll tell a strike by the action of the tip..."

The fog was lifting, grey wisps ran before them over the water and vanished, and the swirling eddies were pink and silver in the slow, strange dawn. The dim shape of another boat loomed out of nowhere and headed toward them in the smoky light. Bill pulled on his port oar and turned the nose in time. He stared at Janet silently as the two boats passed within a few feet of each other. Lila waved her arm pleasantly and pointed to her own rod and shook her head. The figures in the boat blurred in the fog, and then grew sharp again as Bill circled and headed back toward her once more, trolling the quiet water.

"Did you feel a strike?" the Professor asked suddenly.

She gazed blankly at the tip of her rod, dipping and rising regularly. Abruptly it lowered a couple of inches, pointing toward the water like a divining rod, and she felt a very slight tension on her line. The rod ceased to nod. She raised the tip instinctively, and the weight on the line increased. Her reel clicked once or twice, and the line began to move out gently. She could scarcely feel the pull against the motion of the boat. Her fingers found the handle of the reel, and she turned it over tentatively. The weight on her line grew stronger. The Professor stopped rowing.

"I think it's only weeds—" she began.

The other boat had drawn nearer as they drifted uncertainly in its path, and Bill swerved and cut around them to avoid collision. She lifted the rod. The drag on her reel clicked warningly several times, and she saw the line cut sideways in the wake of the boat. She was reeling in cautiously as Bill crossed her path. Suddenly she heard Lila utter a sharp cry and saw the tip of her rod duck violently. At the same instant, the reel in Janet's hand came to life with an insane shriek, and the handle whacked her thumb sharply as it began to spin. Her rod bent almost double. Simultaneously she heard Lila's reel howling, saw her rod curved in a tense arc, heard her voice rising angrily: "Take in your line!!"

Janet stared at her in bewilderment. Her reel still spun madly, and she pressed the butt of her jolting rod against her body, grasping it with both hands as the salmon sounded with short vicious jerks. Lila screamed at her again across the little space between the boats.

"Cut it loose! Cut loose, do you hear me? You'll foul my line!"

Janet said slowly, "But it was my strike—"

Both lines went slack, and they wound their reels desperately and lifted their rods as the salmon boiled to the surface. Janet saw a black spade-like tail break the water some fifty yards ahead, broad, powerful, even at that distance too monstrous to be real. It could never be real. She held her breath. The rod twisted in her limp hands as the tyee lashed its tail once, dove again with a heavy swirl of water, turned, and ran. The flying handle of her reel was a blur, the line sang against the current, the uneven strain of her rod sent throbs of pain up her arms to the shoulders. Lila's voice was harsh above the tumult.

"Cut your line! You'll make me lose him! Quick—"

She heard Bill inquire uneasily: "But, Lila, are you sure?" and Lila turned on him furiously: "Don't sit there like a dummy. Cut her line!" The two boats were being drawn perilously close together in the wake of the stampeding salmon. Janet saw Bill's face cloud angrily. He was staring at Lila in silence. "Do something!" she screamed at him.

The Professor leaned forward. "Anther good thing to know about fishing," he murmured to Janet under his breath, "is just the proper moment to sink the gaff...."

She looked at him with a strange smile. Suddenly she lifted a cleaning knife from the bottom of the boat, laid the taut line across the gunwale, and brought the blade of the knife down sharply. Her line parted with a whine, like a broken violin string, and Lila's rod was almost jerked from her hand as the salmon headed in a desperate run toward the middle of the channel. Her whole body was shaking weakly, and there was no strength left in her hand. The rod clattered from her numbed fingers to the floor. The mad rush of the salmon was carrying the other boat in a wide circle, in and out among the scattered boats of the fishing fleet, and she could hear Lila's voice rising irritably: "Quick, the other oar! He's going under the boat!" The dawn had broken, and Janet could see her plainly as she fought the fish, working it slowly toward her. The boat swung almost alongside again as the fish wallowed feebly to the surface at last. Lila began to lead it in triumphantly, foot by foot. Its silver shoulders were half out of water, and it rolled over helplessly on its side, sweeping its broad tail in vain. Its nose made a little wave as she reeled it steadily toward her. Bill rose with the gaff. Lila shouted to him: "Look out!"

"Shut up!" Bill replied savagely. He lunged at the water, hooked the point of the gaff accurately in a shoulder, sunk his fingers beneath the gills, and hauled it over the side.

They could see its jaw clearly as it flopped into the boat. They cold see the barb of Lila's hook, locked securely in a link of the swivel on the end of Janet's spoon. They saw her own barb, buried solidly in the gristle of the salmon's gaping jaw. The red bead winked at them briefly in the sun...

"—because I want to get one with both of us in it," Janet said in a low voice. "You wouldn't mind snapping it, would you, Professor?"

"I should be delighted," said the Professor gravely.

His face was very sober as he gazed into the finder of the camera. Bill stood on one side of the fifty-pound tyee that dangled from the scales, his big fists rammed into the slanting pockets of his whites, his lower lip protruding slightly in a sheepish grin as he looked at Janet. She stood erect on the other side of the fish, grasping the rod in her hand, her flushed facc full toward the camera. The Professor turned the thumb-screw of the camera, and the focus grew sharper. He could see Janet's eyes wavering as she stole a glance at Bill. The Professor blinked at them mildly.

"Step back a little," he said, motioning with his hand. "Stand behind the fish. It makes it look larger in the picture. That's another good thing to know about fishing..."

Corey Ford Archives, courtesy of Dartmouth College .

Corey with Alastair MacBain, fishing in Canada in the 1930s. These were Corey's Hollywood years, when he was writing screenplays such as Topper Takes a Trip *and* Kodiak.

Corey Ford Archives, courtesy of Dartmouth College .

Corey's twenties were America's, too—the Roaring Twenties. Fishing was his escape even then, when he wrote for Vanity Fair, Life, *and a then-fledgling magazine called* The New Yorker.

Dan Holland, a lifelong hunting and fishing partner of Corey's, was widely considered one of the greatest fly fishermen in the country. The son of Field & Stream's *legendary editor-in-chief, Ray P. Holland, he was the magazine's fishing editor for many years, as well as the author of several books on the sport.*

Corey and his guide during his Canadian/Alaskan adventure where he traveled by train—and horse—as here, through the Canadian Rockies near Jasper.

Corey, again with Alastair MacBain (second from right), on one of the many fishing trips he would take during his life—to the unspoiled lakes and streams of Alaska.

Thirteen

It's a Matter of Principle

*W*hat I want to know: Who gets the girl? Because when you make a wager between gentlemen isn't that supposed to be all there is to it? When it's all agreed ahead of time and all?

It isn't so much the girl, I tell Joe. It's the principle of the thing.

Not that I mean to belittle Ann Marie. Nobody can belittle Ann Marie. Ann Marie waits on tables here at the fishing lodge where we are staying. Ann Marie is the daughter of Mrs. Labbe who runs the lodge and who, I am reasonably certain, would not dress over three hundred pounds. (Joe and I have a bet about that, too.) Ann Marie takes after her mother in several ways, mostly sideways, but you overlook certain things when you have been away on a fishing trip for a couple of weeks without seeing anybody. Besides, Ann Marie doesn't actually wobble like her mother yet—she just sways. She has nice legs and likes to dance and she is young and buxom and really quite attractive, especially if her teeth met.

But it is more than a question of whether Joe takes Ann Marie to the dance in St. Pierre tonight, or I do. It is the principle involved, I tell Joe. Because, I say, the principle involved is sometimes more important than a wager itself, particularly if you have been arguing the principle back and forth as long we have.

Mind you, I like Joe. I think a great deal of Joe. I have been fishing partners with Joe for a number of years, and there is only one thing about Joe: Joe is not strictly a dry fly fisherman. I wouldn't go so far as to say that Joe is a worm fisherman, but I do say that if a worm were to crawl up while Joe wasn't looking and wrap itself around Joe's hook, Joe would not take it off. Joe simply hasn't got the proper attitude toward worms. "What's wrong with a worm?" Joe asks. "It seems to me the least you could do for a fish before you knock it off is to give it a square meal instead of just a bunch of feathers."

I mention this only to show how important it is to get the whole thing settled once and for all.

"Look, Joe," I tell him, "the dry fly fisherman is a sportsman. He sets himself certain standards. He lives up to the rules. It is not a matter of catching fish..."

"Then what's he fishing for?" asks Joe.

"Look, Joe," I begin again, "it's a matter of principle. A dry fly fisherman uses only the most delicate tackle, the lightest leaders, the tiniest barbs. He spots a rising fish, and he casts his fly over it, and he works the fly very carefully so as to simulate the natural action of an insect on the water..."

"And in the meantime," says Joe, "the fish is taking a worm."

"Look, Joe," I tell him, "A dry fly under the right conditions is the most effective lure..."

"Want to make a bet?" says Joe.

This has been going on for years—only, during the past couple of weeks, it has been going on worse than usual. During the past couple of weeks we have had a lot of rain. We have had almost nothing else but rain. The streams are over their banks, the water is roily and full of food washed down by the rain, and the fish are just lying on the bottom with their mouths open and their eyes shut. Naturally you can't do business with a dry fly when the water is like that, I tell Joe. But you can't tell Joe.

"If a dry fly is the most effective lure," he asked me pointedly this morning, helping himself to another slice of fried trout from the platter before him, "why are you having scrambled eggs for breakfast again?"

"Look, Joe," I began once more, "you know perfectly well you can't work a dry fly in the pouring rain..."

The kitchen door swung open wide and Ann Marie entered with a tray of coffee. "Mom says the rain has stopped," she announced cheerfully.

"Well?" Joe grinned at me.

"Look, Joe," I said, "you know perfectly well you can't do a thing when the fish aren't rising..."

"Mom says the fish are rising," said Ann Marie, pouring the coffee. "She says she can see them from the kitchen window. She says you'd better hurry."

"Look, Joe," I said feebly, "you know perfectly well that unless conditions are right...."

"Mom says it's going to be a nice day," Ann Marie interrupted, bending way over and reaching across the table for the sugar bowl. She had on a low-necked dress, and was really quite attractive, especially if she didn't have her hair in rollers. "I'm glad," she added innocently, "because they're having a dance in town tonight."

"Well?" Joe persisted, grinning at me. I did not like his grin. "Want to make a little bet?"

"You're on," I retorted. "My dry fly takes a bigger fish than your worm."

"Mom says," continued Ann Marie bending over again and reaching past us for the cream pitcher, "that I could go to the dance tonight if somebody was to take me."

We both looked at Ann Marie, and then I looked at Joe, and he looked at me.

"And the winner," I said, "takes Ann Marie..."

I began to be sorry about the bet as soon as I saw the river. The water was still high and impossible to wade. It rushed past us in a yellow flood, full of sticks and clumps of grass turning and twisting in the current. A dry fly didn't have a chance, I knew, but it was too late to back out now. Joe grinned. "Don't forget," he taunted, "it's the principle of the thing." He began to work his way out along a fallen hemlock that bobbed and rode the current, and I wandered alone downstream. I glanced back once over my shoulder. He had clambered like a squirrel to the very end of the hemlock and was dunking a large gob of worms in the water. He waved to me genially.

I began to be sorrier and sorrier about the bet as the hours went by. My meager catch lay on the bank, a couple of withered little trout drying and curling in the afternoon sun. An occasional good fish was turning far out in the middle of the stream, but there wasn't a prayer of getting out to them. I stuck a wading boot tentatively into the water, and the force of the current nearly knocked me off balance. I stepped back and surveyed the prospect hopelessly.

At the bottom of the long run, I saw a snag of dead branches and driftwood that had caught on a protruding boulder, some hundred feet from shore, deflecting the main current a little. The swift water swerved inshore, making a little eddy flecked with foam before it straightened out again and raced headlong toward the boiling rapids at the foot of the run. You could see the white waves leaping above the rim of the falls, and a fine spray drifted back toward me on the upstream breeze. The eddy was my only chance. I balanced on a rock and made a couple of experimental casts.

"Are these all you got?" inquired a voice behind me.

I checked my cast and turned. Ann Marie was regarding my fish with interest. She had on a tight black silk dress, silk stockings, and high-heeled pumps. All-in-all she was very attractive, especially if she didn't have so much powder on her face.

"Hurry up and catch something," she shouted above the roar of the falls. "We got to start for the dance pretty soon now."

"You better run upstream," I said resignedly, "and tell Joe..."

In the center of the eddy beside a revolving patch of foam, I thought I saw a fin cut the water. I watched. There was a tiny bump on the water and a swirl. I stripped a couple of lengths of line from the reel and gathered them in my left hand as I began to work the rod, feeding out more and more line until I could drop the fly over the exact spot where I had seen the rise. It drifted downstream a few feet and drowned. I retrieved it with a flick of the rod and sent the line back and then forward again. The fly settled on the water just above the rise, floating down rapidly toward the spot. I began to strip in the slack line as fast as I could to check the drag of the water.

I thought I heard a shriek behind me, but I could not be sure with the deafening boom of the falls in my ear. I turned my head, reeling in the drowned fly. I heard it again, unmistakable this time, and I saw Ann Marie scrambling down the bank toward me, waving her hands.

"Quick!" She pointed toward the stream. "Joe..."

He was turning and twisting out in midstream, borne helplessly by the current. He still clutched his rod in his left hand and beat the water feebly with his right. His head went under once and came up again, and he yelled something, but of course I could not hear him above the thunder of the falls. He was being carried toward them fast. I pointed desperately toward the snag in the middle of the stream; I don't know whether he saw me or not, but as he came abreast of it, he just managed to grab a protruding branch. He swung around, got his free arm around a larger branch, and held on. The water raced past him; he lay stretched out full-length in the current, still clinging dazedly to his rod, his boots bobbing below him. The snag began to shift dangerously with his added weight.

"What are we going to do?" moaned Ann Marie.

"Get a rope," I yelled.

"Rope?"

"A long rope," I said. "Long enough to reach out there."

"But...how are you going to get it to him?"

"I'll take care of that," I said. "Hurry up; that snag isn't going to hold together much longer."

Already a few smaller twigs had broken loose and were speeding downstream; the thing was breaking up fast. I stood on the rock and made a few tentative casts in the air. I began to strip off more line, feeding it out through the guides as I lengthened my cast—forty feet, fifty, sixty. The rod dipped, straightened, dipped again with the weight of my line. It traveled forward and back behind me, and then checked suddenly as the fly caught in a clump of willow. Cursing, I ran back and loosened the fly. A large section of hemlock root suddenly broke loose from the snag and was yanked downstream by the heavy current. For a moment, I thought the whole works would go. I gathered up the slack line, looped it in my hand, and began to feed it out once more. Fifty feet, sixty, seventy. Bit by bit the line lengthened in mid-air. This time I remembered to keep my backcast high. Eighty feet. Joe was hanging on desperately, his head almost under water. Eighty-five.

"I got the rope," Ann Marie panted, running back toward me.

I braced my legs, stripped another loop of line from the reel, made a final cast, and lowered the tip of the rod. The fly traveled out across the stream—I had the wind with me—and dropped onto the snag. At once the weight of the current caught the sunken line and yanked it downstream. The fly flicked off the pile of driftwood and trailed across Joe, and then, just as I had given up hope, its barb embedded itself in the shoulder of Joe's wool shirt.

He knew what to do. Cautiously, trying not to put too great a strain on the delicate leader, he worked the line toward him with his fingers, an inch at a time. He grabbed it and, with a quick gesture, took two turns around his wrist. A branch swept past him, barely missing the taut line.

With trembling fingers I whipped out my knife and cut the line from the reel. Out of the corner of my eye, I saw another piece of driftwood topple from the pile and boil downstream toward the falls. I fastened the end of the line securely to the rope and waved an arm to Joe.

He began to pull it toward him, slowly but surely. Ann Marie and I fed it across the water, a little at a time, lest the weight of the rope itself should drag the whole snag loose. It seemed to take hours, though I suppose it was only a matter of minutes. My legs were hollow. At last I saw the far end of the rope emerge from the water, like a charmed snake, and climb up to Joe's hand. He took a new grip on the branch and ducked under, rolling as he went. When he bobbed up, the rope was around his waist. He knotted it securely.

"Run up the bank," I yelled to Ann Marie, "and make it fast to a tree."

"I can't," said Ann Marie. "It won't reach."

I stared—aghast. There were only a few yards of rope to spare; the nearest tree was well out of range. I thought I heard a cry from the river and I turned. The main section of the snag was tilting upward slowly; the whole thing began to slide off the boulder. I gave Ann Marie a violent push. She staggered backward three or four steps and sat down heavily in the mud.

"Dig in your heels," I shouted.

Percy Crosby was a friend of Corey's from his early life. This cartoon was published in 1928.

I flung myself down and gripped the rope. There was a sudden tug and I felt myself being dragged down the bank toward the river. Then the rope straightened and snubbed taut. Ann Marie was sitting tight.

Lying flat on my back, I could just make out Joe's head swinging around at the end of the rope in a quarter-circle. The pull slackened as he swept into the slower current of the eddy. "Pull!" I gasped to Ann Marie. We began to scramble backward up the bank, hauling on the rope. Joe completed the arc and his feet found solid ground, at last.

*H*is eyes were open as I reached him, and he nodded weakly. I grabbed his free hand and helped him out of the stream. Water ran down his face and out of his sleeves and the pockets of his coat. He crawled toward me on his hands and knees, still dragging his battered rod behind him. With a final effort, he heaved himself onto the bank. He lifted his rod. At the end of his line, firmly impaled on the hook, was an enormous rainbow trout. Joe opened his mouth, emitting a sizable quantity of water, and grinned.

"Well?" he said feebly.

Our progress back to the lodge was rather slow. Joe's clothes trailed water and his boots made a sloshy sound as he walked. My own legs were still a little weak. Ann Marie moved down the trail ahead of us, the

rear of her black skirt plastered with mud. "We've got to hurry," she called over her shoulder. "It's late now."

Joe grinned. "I'll be ready," he told her, "as soon as I get some dry clothes on."

"Wait a minute," I said suddenly. "You'll be ready for what?"

"For the dance," said Joe.

I halted. "You're not taking Ann Marie to the dance."

Joe halted. "I thought we made a bet."

"That's what I mean," I said.

"All right," said Joe, "and who caught the fish?"

"All right," I said, "and who landed it?"

"Come on," said Ann Marie impatiently.

"All right," said Joe, "but if it hadn't been for my worm—"

"All right," I said, "if it hadn't been for my dry fly—"

"Come on, will you?" said Ann Marie. "You can argue later."

"All I want to know," I said, "is who was on the other end hauling it in?"

"All I want to know," said Ann Marie, suddenly beginning to sob, "is who's taking me to the dance? I'm sick and tired of this whole thing. All I got out of it so far is my bloomers wet."

"You're not going to stand there and tell me," Joe continued, ignoring her, "that any fish in his right mind would prefer a bunch of feathers—"

"Look, Joe," I began, "under the proper conditions the most effective lure—"

My voice faded. Joe was gazing past me with a stunned expression. I turned and stared. The trail was empty. Ann Marie had gone. I looked at Joe, and Joe looked at me.

"Well," said Joe slowly, picking up the fish.

"Of course," I told Joe as we started up the trail. "It's really the principle of the thing..."

But just the same, we'd sort of like to know: Who got the girl?

– *Fourteen* –

Herbert's Helper

Why do I like this story, you ask? I'm dying to tell you. Let's call this a period piece—"period" because it's written during a gentler time, a time not so long ago when men opened doors for women and stood up when a lady entered a room. It was written during those halcyon days when a man took off his hat in the company of a lady, and sent her flowers for no reason except "because," and murmured, "I love you" at unexpected times, times that invariably entwined the lovers in a passionate embrace as the strains of "Some Enchanted Evening" climaxed to a crescendo. Men were men and women were feminine and it was...it was...well, I don't know what it was. But it sure ain't today.

In "Herbert's Helper," see what happens to one poor jerk who fails to behave as a gentleman should—and what price he pays for his negligence.

Let this be a lesson to all guys.

*N*ope. No, thanks. Not for me.

You fellows go right ahead, of course. I'll sit here and watch you. Make mine just plain water.

No, I'm off the stuff for good. Haven't touched it for a year, in fact. Just a year ago this May...

I suppose you'll be out there on the stream for the evening rise? You've got plenty of time. Last night the hatch didn't start till after eight. I've seen some hatches here in the old days that didn't get going much before nine or ten o'clock, when it would be so dark we couldn't see the tips of our rods, and we'd stand up to our hips in that black water and play the trout from memory. Sometimes we wouldn't get back to the clubhouse till midnight, and we'd all meet upstairs in somebody's room and put our feet on the bed and break out a bottle...

Not any more, though. You couldn't hire me to touch it now, not after what happened. Never again for me.

No, fellows, I'm afraid I wouldn't know where to tell you to go tonight. You see, the stream isn't what it used to be. It's all different now. I went down to Cemetery Pool the other day; it's the first time I've been back there since The Old Boy's been gone, and they've built a public picnic ground in that birch grove right beside the stream, with stone fireplaces and neat green cans labeled "Refuse" and even a springboard out over the deepest part. It gave me a funny feeling, like seeing the house where I used to live torn down. I got to thinking about picnickers throwing eggshells and crusts of bread into The Old Boy's pool and kids diving down around his favorite ledge, and I came away without even wetting a line.

It just isn't the same stream any more.

Yeah, that's the Old Boy, over the mantel. Seven pounds, thirteen and three-quarters ounces—he'd have gone eight pounds easy if he'd been weighed right away. It's right there on the nameplate. We all chipped in and had it engraved, with the weight and under it just, "The Old Boy." That's all. No name of the lucky angler, nothing else, just the date. May 13...

He looks natural, don't you think? They did a good job of mounting him in New York. I took him down to the city myself to make sure they got it right. The taxidermist wanted to touch him up a little, patch his fins in a couple of places and give him a nice long, tapering waistline, but I told him The Old Boy was no youngster any more, he was old and dumpy and all his weight was down around his hips. He had a big, solid tail and a belly like an alderman and a thick neck with baggy rolls of fat around his gills and under his chin. I made them leave the fins all chewed and battered, and the scar in his side where somebody gaffed him once, and that great ugly hook of a snout with three or four pieces of steel broken off deep in the bone. I stood over them until they got the right expression on his face. I wanted that same mean look I've seen in his eye when he'd roll over once and drown my fly and then sink down again to the bottom of the pool, with a cold, superior smile, like a bank president turning down a third mortgage. I bet I looked over a thousand eyes the taxidermist had in a drawer before I found one that was mean enough.

I guess I knew The Old Boy better than anybody else, I'd been fishing for him so many years. Maybe you'll think I'm crazy, but I believe he finally got to know me, too. There would be an expression on his face when I rose him and he saw who it was that was different from the way he'd look at Judge Conacher, or Doc Marston, or any of the others. It's like two old enemies that have been fighting each other so long, there gets to be something between them that nobody else can understand. It's even closer than what's between two friends. I don't know, but it happens.

It's funny to look up at him now and realize he's gone. I used to set my desk calendar by The Old Boy. I'd spend all winter figuring out new ways to get my fly past that swift run in the center of the stream, and every spring I'd be at Cemetery Pool on opening day—sleet or snow—it didn't matter, just to try him again. He got to be more than a fish with me. He was a religion. I'd talk about him, think about him, dream about him. Sometimes I'd lie awake for hours, staring at the ceiling and planning the day when I'd land him at last, how I'd stroll back here to the clubhouse with The Old Boy in my arms, and I'd lay him down on the dining room table without a word, and just fold my arms and stand there smiling modestly while everybody raved and pounded my back and poured out the drinks...

Not any more, though. I found out I couldn't handle it. I always say it's all right if you can handle it, but when something happens, well, it's time to swear off. I haven't touched a drop since I broke off with Estelle...

Thanks, fellows. I guess you saw in the papers. I appreciate your saying that, but as a matter of fact I can be sensible about the whole thing now. I admit it hit me hard when it happened, but now I can see it was probably the best thing all around. She and Charlie Werner are very happy; they're expecting a youngster pretty soon, and its middle name is going to be Herbert: Charles Herbert Werner. If it's a boy, that is. But Stell says it will be a boy, and she's always right.

Naturally I don't blame Charlie. I don't want you to think I have any hard feelings toward him at all. Charlie's a fine fellow; I really think the world of him, the only thing I ever had against him was the fact the he didn't seem to have quite the same attitude toward fishing as the rest of us at the club. I happen to know that once in a while Charlie fishes wet, and personally I've always felt that a man who would fish with a wet fly would be just as apt to use some other kind of artificial lure, like a spinner, and someday, if a man like that should happen to lose his spinner, it would be the most natural thing in the world for him to reach down and put on a hellgramite instead, and from a hellgramite, only one more step to using a worm. Of course, I only mention this to show that Charlie never really had the spirit of this club at heart. Otherwise he's one of the best fellows I know. We're very good friends, and when he and Estelle came back from England after their honeymoon, he brought me a three-ounce Marmoset rod that's got the sweetest action you ever felt.

I don't know why I've never used that rod.

*I*t was through Charlie that I met Estelle. They'd been going around together a couple of years, nothing much, and one night he introduced me to her at a dance. Well, it was just like that. It was all over before either of us knew what was happening. I said to her, "How do you do, Miss Baird?" and she said to me, "How do you do, Mr. Hatch?" but I might just as well have said, "Will you marry me?" and she might just as well have said, "Yes." We stalled around a week or two before we announced our engagement, but it really happened the very first time we looked into each other's eyes. I guess it was one of those things.

I was pretty ripe for something to happen, at that. It must have been in the back of my mind for some time. You know how it is when you start crowding forty, and you notice you're letting out the waistband of your trousers a little more each year, and the barber tells you that place on top is no more than holding its own, and all of a sudden it occurs to you that all restaurant food tastes the same; or one night when you get back to the hotel after a month's vacation, the doorman sees your suitcase and says, "Are you leaving, sir?" That's when you stop and think how nice it would be to have somebody to fuss over you, and put your things away where they belong, and sit on the arm of your chair at night and take your cigarette out of your mouth and knock off the ashes and put it back in your mouth for you again. And the next thing you know, it's happened.

Estelle was just the right girl for me, of course. Everybody said so. They all said I was pretty lucky to grab a sensible girl like Estelle, instead of some butterfly type. There was nothing flighty about Estelle. I don't mean she couldn't enjoy herself, but she never drank cocktails or acted silly, and it was always Estelle that drove the car home. You could depend on Estelle. She was as pretty as a picture, like one of those old-fashioned silhouette pictures you used to see, with perfect features, like they'd been cut out with a pair of scissors, and a straight nose and a sharp little chin. She had a mind of her own, and everybody said that was just what I needed. I'm inclined to change my mind now and then, but once Stell decided something, she'd go through with it. What's more, she'd be right.

*L*ike for instance about fishing. She knew how I felt about fishing, and she was very sweet about the whole thing. She said the last thing on earth she wanted to do was to interfere with my pleasure in any way. She said she knew how much fishing meant to me, and she was perfectly willing to take a backseat, as she put it, and let me fish whenever I wanted to. She said a husband should enjoy his own hobbies, and all she ever wanted to do was encourage him. She said we were going to be more than sweethearts, we were going to be pals. "I'm not going to nag and fret and mope around by myself when you go fishing," she said. "I'm not going to stay home and worry whether you've wrecked the car or caught your death of cold or fallen in and gotten drowned."

"That's right, honey," I smiled, patting her. "No sense sitting there and brooding."

"Of course not," she said. "I'm going to come along with you."

"You are?" I said. Maybe there was something about the way I said it.

"Oh, don't worry, Herbie," she laughed gaily. "I'm not going to *fish*. I'll just sit on the bank and watch. I'll hand you the net when you need it, and light your pipe, and at night I'll put your tackle away where it belongs. Like a partner, dear," she whispered, looking up at me and stroking my cheek, "a real fishing pal."

What could I say? I was so much in love with her that I didn't even question the idea. "Why sure, Stell," I said, "of course. You bet."

"I'm going to learn all about fishing," she said. "I'm going to study until I'm really an expert on the subject. I'm going to be an ideal fisherman's wife."

And she was, too. It wasn't her fault. The only trouble is that there's no such thing as an ideal fisherman...

Everything was fine, at first. We'd planned to be married that fall, after fishing season was over and I could devote a little more time to the wedding, and when I headed up here to the Mayfly Club for opening day, she insisted on coming along, too. She said she might as well learn this fishing business right now. She brought along a whole trunkful of books about angling, and she read them from cover to cover. That's one thing about Stell, she's thorough. She studied and studied until she picked up all the technical names and phrases. I used to get a great kick out of hearing her talk. I'll never forget the night she got into an argument with old Judge Conacher at dinner on the comparative merits of the floating versus the sunken leader, and the proper presentation of the fly to a rising trout.

"If the cast is checked just as it straightens," she said, "this will have the effect of throwing the fly downstream, not only presenting the counterfeit to the trout tail first in imitation of the natural insect, but also causing the leader to describe a sharp curve and follow after it in such a way that the angle of its shadow will not strike the retina of the trout's eye."

"I see," said Judge Conacher, mopping his lips with his napkin and looking around a little wildly.

"In fishing the floating fly," she continued, making marks on the tablecloth with her fork, "due allowance must be made for that portion of an imaginary circle enclosing the base of an inverted cone that will not come within view of the fish at the apex—"

"Hrmph!" said Judge Conacher, pushing back his chair suddenly and leaving his dessert half-finished.

Of course she came along every day and watched me fish. She brought a sewing basket filled with yarn and spools of thread, and she'd sit on the bank for hours without a word, as busy as a little chipmunk, while I worked the pool in front of her. I got curious after a while and finally I asked her what she was doing.

"I'm tying flies," she replied with a smile.

"What?" I gasped.

"I cut the patterns out of your catalogue," she said, "I've got a Coachman and a Pink Lady, and I'm just starting on a Parmachenee Belle."

And they weren't bad, either. They were pretty good. The wings had a tendency to fold up like an umbrella, and the hackle was matted like a wrestler's chest, but I've seen lots of worse ties in my time. I was so tickled I could hardly speak. I hugged her and said she was the greatest little partner a fisherman ever had and I was the happiest fellow in the world.

It wasn't till about the middle of the week that I suddenly realized a very funny thing. The thought struck me so hard that I stopped short, right in the middle of the stream, and tried to figure it out. I'd been here three days and I hadn't taken a fish. Not a fish. I couldn't understand it. I didn't know whether my form was off, or I was using the wrong patterns, or it was just a run of bad luck. I was so worried I even mentioned it to Estelle.

"As a matter of fact," she said frankly, "I've been watching you and I think you're fishing too long a line."

I lowered my rod and stared at her, a little taken aback.

"Your line drowns and causes an unnatural drag on your fly," she explained. "According to the experts, a twenty-five foot cast is sufficient in a strong current, and the line should be stripped with the left hand to keep pace with the speed of the floating fly."

"Oh," I said, a little irritated. I admit I'm not the best fisherman in the world, but I don't like to admit anybody else is either. "I suppose the experts would do it like this."

I made a very short cast, about fifteen feet in front of me, and a sixteen-inch brownie rose immediately and smacked it so hard he took away fly and all.

I didn't say much to her as we wandered down the stream. The day suddenly seemed very hot and disagreeable, the insects were more annoying than usually, and even Cemetery Pool, ahead of us around the bend, was flat and lifeless in the steamy sunlight. I left her on the bank and crossed the shallow riffles at the tail of the pool and worked my way cautiously back up the other side through the tangled hemlocks and grey birch until I could worm out onto the ledge of rock directly above the pool. I lay there on my stomach for a moment or two to let my eyes get accustomed to the glare.

The Old Boy was there. I could just make him out among the undulating shadows on the bottom of the pool. He was lying very still, his gills hardly moving, just his body lifting and falling with the slight current and his dorsal fin waving back and forth gently, like a fat lady rocking and fanning herself on a veranda. I made a couple of half-hearted casts over him, but I knew it wasn't much use. The Old Boy was stubborn and cranky, and if he didn't feel like rising, there was nothing short of dynamite that could make him budge. You simply had to be still and wait him out.

"Do you see anything?" Estelle shouted from the opposite bank.

I held up my hand for silence, but it was too late. She was climbing down the bank toward the stream, and her foot dislodged a little pebble. It hit the water with a tiny *clunk*. Slowly, without any sign of motion, The Old Boy began to pull back, tail first, retiring under the ledge with the solid dignity of an elderly club member sinking into his favorite leather chair behind the Sunday *Times*. He simply withdrew, and a moment later there was only the green apron of rock, with the moss wavering in the current and the flecks of mica glinting in the sun. I reeled in my line and waded back across the stream in silence.

"Maybe you were using the wrong fly," Estelle suggested brightly.

"It isn't the fly, Stell," I explained, controlling myself. I was using my favorite fly, a regulation number fourteen Whirling Blue Dun, standard tie, starling wings and ginger hackle and mole fur body with a couple of turns of flat gold tinsel at the end. I've always claimed if I were ever cast on a desert island with just one trout fly...but to get back to what I was saying. "After all, dear," I told her, "I've been putting this same fly over The Old Boy for years—"

"You never caught him," she pointed out.

I let that pass.

"Because I have a little something here I just tied," she said. "I worked it out myself, and I bet it will take The Old Boy. I've named it 'Herbert's Helper.'"

Fellows, I'm not going to try to describe that fly. I'm sorry, but I can't tell you about it even now. All I can say is that it looked like one of those salads that women get up out of the leftovers of a bridge party. I remember it had green eyes, and a sort of peacock tail, and the body looked like the license plates on a cross-country bus, and all it needed was somebody walking in front of it swinging a red lantern. I held it gingerly by one wing and dropped it into my fly box.

"It's very pretty, Estelle," I said. "It's quite an idea, honey, and now it's getting kind of hot, and we've been fishing all day, and maybe it would be better if we just got back to the Club and rested up a little before supper..."

Charlie Werner was sitting all alone in the living room when we got back, playing solitaire. I went over to him and lowered my voice. "Look, Charlie," I said, "there's sort of a little favor you could do for me tonight, if you're not going fishing."

"Sure, Herbie," he said, looking up from the cards.

"It's Estelle," I said. "I mean, she hasn't gone anywhere lately, and I thought it might be nice if you took her to the movies or something, just for a change—"

"Of course, old man," said Charlie with a sort of an odd expression. I didn't think anything of it at the time. "I'm always glad to do a favor for you, Herb, you know that."

"By the way, Charlie," I added, "I wouldn't say anything to her about my asking you, see? I mean, I think she'd like it better if it came from you."

"Don't you worry," said Charlie, "I'll take care of everything all right, Herb."

There was a rather small hatch of flies that night. I stood on the bank of Cemetery Pool, smoking my pipe and watching the swarm of insects beating their way upstream, dropping one by one onto the water and skittering downstream on their tails until a trout rushed to the surface and gobbled them down. The pool was alive with little fish, leaping and slapping, but I wasn't looking at them. I was looking at that black, silent run of water over against the ledge. I was watching a suspicious little bulge that seemed to swell and flatten again, quite regularly, in the center of the run. I could feel the goose-pimples stand out suddenly all over me, and my mouth tasted dry and I swallowed hard. That bulge meant just one thing: The Old Boy had started to rise.

My hands shook so that I could hardly set up my rod. I waded out to my ankles, made a couple of false casts, and shot the line toward the ledge. I suppose I was overeager. Just as I sent it forward, there was a sharp check behind me and then the line rained down all over me in a heap. My fly and half my leader still dangled from the branch of a hemlock overhead. I swore a little, reached in my pocket for the old leather wallet where I keep my extra leaders, and opened it hurriedly. My heart dropped with a distinct thump. The wallet was empty. I looked through all my pockets. I looked in my fly boxes. I even looked inside the band of my hat. My leaders weren't there. I didn't have so much as a strand of gut on me, and the hatch was fading fast. Already the bulge over by the farther bank was appearing less and less often. I knew there would be no time to drive all the way to the clubhouse and back again. I lowered my rod, waded out of the pool, and climbed the bank to the car.

*E*stelle didn't get back until nearly eleven that night. She and Charlie were laughing together pleasantly as they entered the living room, but as soon as she saw my face, she stopped laughing and came over and took my hand. "Herbert," said asked, "what's happened, dear?"

"What's been keeping you?" I demanded, trying to make my voice sound steady. "I've been pacing this room for two solid hours—"

"Did you miss me that much, Herbie?" she murmured happily, and there was a soft light in her eye.

"You bet I did," I said. "I was nearly crazy." I braced myself. "Where in hell did you put my leaders?"

The light went out of her eye, and suddenly her voice sounded very flat. "So that was why you missed me?"

"Listen, Estelle," I explained to her, a little shaky, "The Old Boy was rising tonight. Do you know what that means? He was rising, and I wanted a leader, and I looked in my leather wallet where I always keep them and it was empty. They weren't there. They were gone. Somebody had taken them—"

"I put them away," she said stiffly. "I put them all in that black metal box where they belong. The one marked 'Leaders.'"

Of course, that was the one place I hadn't thought of looking, but it didn't make me feel any better. I waited a moment to get calm. "Estelle," I said at last, "I think from now on I'd prefer not to have you meddle around my tackle any more. I wish next time you'd kindly leave my things alone."

"But I was only trying—" Suddenly her voice broke and she turned and started upstairs. "All right, Herbert," she said over her shoulder, "if...if that's the way you feel about it..."

She mounted the stairs and went down the hall to her room. I stood there watching her, feeling pretty miserable, but she didn't look back, and I went upstairs to my own room and slammed the door. I lay awake a long time staring at the ceiling. It was the first time we hadn't said good-night since we were first engaged....

The next day was one of those days that comes just once in a fin. The sky was overcast and milky-white, the hills were bright blue and they looked very near, and everything was so still you could hear the river distinctly, running below the clubhouse. You could almost smell the damp rocks. I knew The Old Boy would be up today if he ever was. Charlie was sitting on the railing of the porch enjoying the morning air, and I hesitated a moment and glanced around to make sure nobody heard me.

"Well, Charlie," I asked him off-hand, "planning to try a little fishing?"

"I hadn't thought," said Charlie.

"Because I was only going to suggest if you weren't," I said, avoiding his eye, "Estelle is very fond of golf and I know she'd enjoy it if you took her down to Livingston Manor and shot a couple of rounds this morning. I wouldn't mention it," I added, "except, of course, there probably won't be anything doing out there on the stream..."

"Sure, I'd be glad to," said Charlie. "I feel just like a little golf."

"You can sort of explain to her when she comes downstairs, I said with an anxious glance in the direction of the stream. "Just tell her I'd have gone along myself only I don't play golf, and I thought I'd just wander down to the pool instead and maybe try a couple of casts."

"I'll tell her, Herb," Charlie promised soberly as I started for the car. "I'll see she understands."

The last morning mists had risen by the time I reached Cemetery Pool and the surface of the water was flat and calm. Even the black run of water beside the ledge glided past without a ripple, and there wasn't so much as a chub rising anywhere in the pool. I made a few short casts as I worked out into the deeper water and set my Blue Dun lightly on the very edge of the swift current. It rode the whole distance without a fault, standing on its hackle with its wings cocked perfectly, and I retrieved it as it swung around at the end of the cast and put it out again, a little nearer the ledge. It ran the field once more without interference. With my heart in my mouth, I lengthened my cast and laid it accurately at the very edge of the rocks and watched it as it rocked and dipped down the fast run of bumpy water, right over The Old Boy's nose. Nothing. I tried a few feet away on either side; I tried above the ledge and then below it; I tried the eddy at the head of the pool and the foam-flecked backwater, and even the nearer bank. Nothing. I worked the swirl of whitewater at the head of the stretch, and the twin boulders on either side of the swift, and the dead water above them. Still nothing. My arm ached, my hatband was wet with perspiration, my eyes had begun to throb; but there was nothing doing. The Old Boy simply wasn't there.

I must have fished for about an hour when I heard a sudden scrabbling behind me and a large rock rolled own the bank and landed in the water at my feet with a solid splash. I whirled around to shout and checked myself as Estelle's face appeared through the alders, tear-stained and contrite.

"You go right ahead, dear," she called demurely. "I won't disturb you."

I watched the ripples from the stone widening out slowly across the pool.

"I'll be very quiet," Estelle assured me, clambering down the bank and dislodging a couple more stones in the process. "I promise not to even say a word."

"I thought you were going to play golf with Charlie," I said.

"I had to talk to you, darling," she said with a sob in her voice. "I just had to tell you I was so sorry about last night and I promise never, never to touch your things again. But now I'm not going to talk any more," she frowned to herself. "I'm just going to sit here and watch you fish."

I waded out into the pool again and began to put my fly over the smooth water by the ledge, but my casting seemed to get sloppier and sloppier. A couple of times I slapped the water hard behind me, and once the fly nicked the tip of my rod. I could feel Estelle's eyes on the back of my neck and it made me self-conscious and stiff in all my movements. I knew I looked as clumsy as an amateur, and I began to wish she would say something and get it over with. The suspense was unbearable. I almost shouted with relief when she broke the silence at last.

"Herbert."

"What is it?"

"Why don't you try around that old snag at the bottom of the pool?" she suggested. "It looks like a pretty good place."

I knew the water was shallow there and there would be nothing but chubs, but, after all, there was nothing to lose. Besides, I felt a little sorry about last night and this seemed to be an easy way to make amends. I whipped the Blue Dun through the air once or twice to dry it and cast it toward the pile of driftwood over against the far bank. The current sucked it out of sight, and when I tried to retrieve it, it was fast.

"Now I'm hung up," I muttered reproachfully.

I gave a quick tug but the fly refused to come loose. I started to walk toward it, mumbling things under my breath. In order to free it, I'd have to wade right through the best part of the pool and that would end my fishing for the day. I clambered onto a submerged boulder and lifted my rod, straining it a little to free the fly. Whatever it was fast to suddenly loosened, and began to drift downstream, pulling the fly with it. I called to Estelle.

"Get down below it in the flat water, dear," I said wearily, "and catch it when it goes by."

"You're certainly calm," said Estelle admiringly, "for anybody that's been trying as long as you have to hook The Old Boy

"Godalmighty," I yelled, and fell off the boulder.

Fortunately, the water was not above my armpits, and I could still hold the rod in the air and work it a little; but the line seemed jammed. As The Old Boy turned and moved off in a slow circle, I had to pay it out of the reel with my hand. I saw at a glance what had happened. My foot had stepped through the slack loop in the line and it was passed around one ankle and between my legs. If The Old Boy swam around me, he would wind me up like a top.

Now, maybe you've never tried to balance yourself on one leg in a swift current and hoist the other leg underwater while holding a rod in the air with one hand, and twisting halfway around while you pass a sunken line around your free foot with the other; but you can see that it would be hard to do and still maintain any kind of proper angling form. My rod wavered and dipped like a tree in a gale, the tip doubled over dangerously as The Old Boy sounded; my reel gave a strangled yelp, and I clamped the butt of the rod beneath my arm and tried to pay out more line with my free hand. Estelle ran back up the bank and shouted something to me.

"What?" I gasped over my shoulder, dropping the line again as I lost my balance and staggered backward a couple of steps.

"Your rod," she screamed. "Hold it vertical."

"Thank you, dear," I said between my teeth, groping around my ankle and trying to find the loop of line I had just dropped. The Old Boy made another run across the pool, and I grabbed again desperately for the reel.

"Give him line," Estelle shouted. "Let him run if he wants."

"Yes, dear," I said, propping my rod in the curve of my chin and picking frantically at a backlash that I had just discovered in the reel. The rod dipped once more and Estelle began to wave her hands.

"Herbert," she shrieked, "watch the curve of your rod. Keep it uniform and let the tip even the strain. It is the action of the tip that keeps the proper tension on the fish at all times—"

The Old Boy swung around in a lazy circle—I don't suppose he had the faintest idea that he was on—and came straight toward me. I tried to back away, tripped over the boulder, ducked down into the water over my chin, and found my footing in the nick of time. I rose again, blowing out like a porpoise, and above the commotion I could still hear Estelle's voice in my ears.

"Don't lower the tip of your rod, Herbert," she was saying. "Don't give him a slack line. He's going to get off!"

I swung around and faced her. "Estelle," I began, "will you please shut the hell up—"

I suppose I must have lowered the rod as I turned. I felt the strain ease all at once and the line went slack. I turned back and stared at it stupidly.

"He's off," said Estelle.

And she was right...

We drove back to the clubhouse in silence. On my honor, I didn't say a word.

Not a single word. At least, I was very careful about that. I left her in the car and went inside and found Charlie sitting in the living room, still playing solitaire. I admit this was an odd thing for Charlie to be doing, when you think of it now, but it seemed the most natural thing in the world at the time. I took out a hundred dollars and laid it on the table.

"Charlie," I said hoarsely, "this is the biggest favor I'll ever ask you. I want you to take my car. I want you to drive Estelle back to New York. I want you to take her to dinner, and the theater, and a nightclub, and give her a whale of a time. I want you to keep her amused. I want you to keep her so amused that she won't be back here until the rest of my vacation is over. Will you do that for me, Charlie?"

"Herb, old man," said Charlie, wringing my hand, "you just leave her to me."

They didn't get all the way to New York, as a matter of fact. They only got as far as Armonk. They sent me a wire from Armonk that they'd stopped off there to be married.

It was about three o'clock in the afternoon when I got the telegram, because the station is only open when the afternoon train goes down, and I sat looking at it for a minute or two before I even grasped what it said. Here I was, a million miles from nowhere, no train, no car, no way of getting down there in time. What could I do? What would you do? What would anybody do?

That's what I did.

I had the fifth of old bourbon that I was saving to celebrate in case I ever landed The Old Boy, and I poured myself a hooker and I read the telegram again. I poured myself another hooker, and I read it over a third time. I thought about Estelle, and I poured myself another shot of bourbon. I thought about what I said to her last night and I poured another shot, and I thought about what I said to her this morning and I poured another shot, and then I thought about Charlie, and I began to drink right out of the bottle without pouring. The more I thought about things, the more I drank, and the more I drank, the more I thought about things. It got so I couldn't tell whether I was drinking or thinking.

I don't remember eating supper. I don't remember much of anything that evening. It got darker and darker and later and later, and people kept coming in and saying something to me, and I'd just shake my head and have another drink. I didn't want to talk to anybody. Finally they went upstairs to bed, but I just sat there all alone. It was a misty night and you could hear the river running in the distance and smell the damp rocks. I thought of The Old Boy and then I thought of Estelle, and I remember opening my fly box and taking out Herbert's Helper. The wings were upside down and the hackle was wound the wrong way, but Estelle had tied it for me with her own little hands and now she was gone forever. I poured myself another drink and I don't remember any more after that...

The next thing I knew was when Doc Marston shook my shoulder and I squinted out of one eye and discovered I was lying in my own bed and it was morning, and my mouth tasted as if somebody had slept in it all night. I tried to turn away, but Doc kept tugging at my arm and shouting something, and finally I peeled open both eyes and stared at him. He was acting so excited that, at first, I was afraid the club was on fire, and then I felt my head and I was afraid it wasn't. Doc hauled me out of bed.

"Come downstairs, quick!" he yelled. "Everybody's waiting!"

I slipped my feet into a pair of moccasins and stumbled downstairs in my pajamas, rubbing my eyes. I could hear excited voices in the kitchen, and I banged into a couple of chairs and fumbled with the knob and pushed open the door. There was a crowd around a table, and they all looked at me and grinned as I entered the room. I stared at the table and then I grabbed a chair to steady myself. It was all over. The Old Boy was lying on some newspapers, his eyes glassy, his big silvery sides shiny and cold.

"Who caught him?" I asked hoarsely.

"Who caught him?" Doc repeated, and everybody laughed and bent over the trout again.

"Just short of eight pounds," Judge Conacher said. "I guess that comes pretty close to being the all-time record in this club—"

"Who caught him?" I repeated in a husky voice.

"All right, Herbie," Doc grinned, "only next time don't hang your wet waders where everybody can see them."

I turned slowly and stared at my wading boots, standing in a little puddle of water behind the stove. "Who's been wearing my waders?"

"Well, I don't know, Herbie," Judge Conacher winked at me, removing something from The Old Boy's jaw, "but I guess it must have been the same fellow that was using your fly."

I looked at the bedraggled fly. It was Herbert's Helper. Estelle was right again...

"Tell us all about it, Herbie," Doc Marston said, pouring a glass of bourbon and setting it in front of me. "I know how long you've been trying to land The Old Boy. I bet it was a thrill you'll never forget."

I shoved the glass away from me. "No, thanks," I said sadly. "Never again..."

Well, you fellows better get started if you want to make that evening rise. You might try Cemetery Pool, there's probably some little two or three-pounders in there. I don't believe I'll be going out tonight. I'm just going to sit here and look at The Old Boy. Sometimes if I look at him long enough, I can almost see his fins begin to move and his gills open and shut again. I wouldn't be surprised if he backed off the plank tail-first and disappeared into the stones of the fireplace. He looks so natural up there...

If only he could talk.

– Fifteen –

Headwaters of the Connecticut

> The Connecticut River, to those of us who call ourselves New Englanders, is nothing more than a bunch of water. It's nothing more than a wide ribbon that crashes between Vermont and New Hampshire, separating them, yet joining the two states like fraternal twins. That makes the Connecticut kind of like a mother—a maternal bunch of water. Moms nourish their children and the Connecticut nourishes hers, too. She nourishes the green pastures that hug her sides; she gives mother's milk to the forest's creatures; and from her womb she delivers fish to the fisherman. Yet she's a breathtaking beauty and dresses up well: At sunrise she glistens and shimmers in the sparkling light of the rising sun, and at dusk she's a dark and mysterious lady, elegant and sultry.
>
> This lady has a past, and Corey tells you all about it in "Headwaters of the Connecticut." She's been around the block and she has her secrets.
>
> Nonetheless, I think you'll find she's one heck of a broad.

Fishermen are by nature a close-mouthed lot and tend to be taciturn to the point of downright rudeness if someone asks the location of a secret fishing hole. But when a fisherman happens to be as fine a painter as Henry McDaniel, artistic instinct may override his sense of prudence as an angler; and so it is that some of his watercolors, should you get the chance to view them, reveal the actual names of some of the best trout pools on the upper Connecticut River.

It may come as a revelation to learn that there are trout in the Connecticut at all. Down Massachusetts way, past the cities of Springfield and Hartford to the Sound, the lower river is polluted and fishless, its concrete banks lined with factories, and its murky current churned by garbage scows. But as you drive north through New Hampshire along Route 10, the water gets clearer and the river grows

narrower and somehow younger with each successive mile, leaping play-
fully over boulders and wandering here and there across the meadows
like an active child until, around Colebrook, it is back in its own childhood again, an ebullient trout stream with shallow riffles and sandbars
and deep, lovely pools—much as it was a century ago, when the Atlantic
salmon came all the way up to these headwaters to spawn.

The salmon are gone forever, but there are still rainbows and squaretails and canny browns to fill the creel of a cannier angler. Stop and fish
the fast water above Lyman's Dam, or work the big Cut Bank Pool at
Colebrook, or wade out into the old Salmon Hole near West Stewartston
until the water gurgles around your boot tops. When the evening hatch is
on, you may see the nose of a big lunker bumping the surface near you,
or smashing savagely at a drifting mayfly, or swirling under your own
floating lure. Follow the river north of Colebrook along Route 3 as the
volume of water slacks off, and you can wade back and forth over the
gravel bars, putting your fly onto a deep run beside the far bank when
you spot a rise. Or travel farther north to Pittsburg, New Hampshire and
gaze with awe into the great pool, right in the heart of town, where last
year the school principal hooked a thirteen-pound brown on a streamer
fly and fought it most of the night while villagers lined the banks and
cheered.

At Pittsburg, a flood-control dam halts the Connecticut abruptly, backing up the water for ten miles in a sluggish artificial lake. Once it was an
enchanted stream, meandering under wooden bridges and through pasture
lands cropped clean for your backcast. In the still evening, the air was
always sweet with wood smoke and fresh-plowed earth, and you could
hear the splash of feeding trout around the bend. Today you can look
down through thirty feet of water, and if the sun is right you can make out
the farms, drowned like the lost Atlantis, and a rippling brown shadow that
might be the old covered bridge beneath which I took a five-pound rainbow on a number sixteen Black Gnat.

But north of this man-made lake, the river comes to life again, a bub-
bling brook now, cascading over huge boulders and halting now and then
in a tranquil pool, studded at dark with little rises. The trout are smaller
here and it isn't easy fishing—the boughs of the overhanging hemlocks
are festooned with broken leaders left there by luckless anglers—but it is
my favorite section. Here the smaller tributaries, Indian Stream and Perry

Stream, flow into the main river; and to the north are the three connecting lakes that are the true origin of the Connecticut. All the river north of Pittsburgh is wisely restricted to fly fishing and is presided over benignly but firmly by New Hampshire's game wardens as though the north country belonged to them.

It is a unique part of New England, this tiny hunk of New Hampshire that butts up rudely through the neat geometric line of the U.S.-Canadian border and pokes its impudent head into Quebec. At the close of the Revolutionary War, the Treaty of Parks established the state's boundary as the "northwestern-most head of the Connecticut River;" but a Yankee surveyor back in 1783 assumed that "head" meant "source," so the international border was set clear west to Hall Stream and all the way north to the Third Connecticut Lake. This liberal usurpation of Canadian real estate was a sore point with our northern neighbor, and in 1827 the two countries decided to submit the whole question to the impartial judgment of the King of Holland.

The King of Holland decided that everything west of the Connecticut River belonged to Quebec, thereupon the United States thanked him coldly for his services and proceeded to ignore him completely. This left the disputed area as a sort of no man's land to which neither side held title. Canadian officers conscripted some indignant New Hampshire citizens for His Majesty's military service, and American customs officials began levying duties on farm products imported from New Hampshire to the United States. So in 1832 the pioneersmen along the upper Connecticut formed their own state called the Indian Stream Republic and seceded from the Union. They wrote a Constitution, organized a standing army of forty men, and for four years the little Republic stood off Canada to the north and the United States to the south, actually engaging in several border skirmishes and taking a few prisoners. These captives presented a problem, since the new Republic didn't have a jail, but the enterprising sheriff solved it by keeping his wards inside a seven hundred pound iron kettle used for making turpentine, which he turned bottomside-up on a flat rock.

Beleaguered on both sides, the Indian Stream Republic finally decided in 1836 to join the United States again and was somewhat discomfited to learn that official Washington wasn't even aware that it had left. Thus ended this country's smallest and shortest-lived republic. Sometimes, when you look at such government benefits as Francis Lake and Murphy Dam, you wish the embattled farmers had held out a little longer.

It has always been a land of rugged individualism. The country north of Colebrook is definitely Canadian in character, dotted with fir and spruce trees. The isolated farms still have wood stoves and handcrank telephones, and the oldtimers speak a pure English direct from the old country—"It rains" instead of "It's raining," and the expression, "S'I" which is an abbreviation of "Says I." Progress hasn't changed it much; there is still the same pioneer feeling about it, the unostentatious hospitality, the primitive beauty. Today its main income is from sportsmen, and there are excellent hostels where the fisherman may stay. You'll find some landlocked salmon on the lakes, and good trout fishing up and down the river as well as in the small feeder-streams and ponds. Deer browse the meadows at night, partridge explode out of the bushes, beavers slap their tails unexpectedly behind you as you fish, and now and then a moose looks down sullenly from the bank.

So rig your rod and explore the upper Connecticut; and if you stumble on a secret pool, don't tell anyone else. It will be your secret, too.

– Sixteen –

Hook, Line, and Sinker

Corey carried on a love affair with Canada and Alaska, and hunted and fished there whenever he could. In "Hook, Line, and Sinker," he relates his exploits fishing for rainbow and salmon, and his brief but eventful membership in the Fish Liars' Club.

I was elected to the Fish Liars' Club in Fairbanks, Alaska. The ceremony was held on the sidewalk outside the Model Restaurant, where I had just purchased a dead grayling to use in a few photographs. In vain I tried to explain that I was not in the habit of buying fish for photographs, that I had caught plenty of grayling myself, that unfortunately I just happened to forget to put any film in my camera. The secretary of the Fish Liars' Club interrupted me solemnly, cast a brief but significant glance at his fellow members gathered about us on the sidewalk, and cleared his throat.

"It gives me great pleasure," he said, tucking my membership card in the band of my fishing hat, "to congratulate you on your unanimous election to the Fish Liars' Club. We have every reason to believe that you will be a credit to the organization."

To be sure, there is nothing very exclusive about the Ancient Order of Fish Liars. Any angler can qualify. The organization bars neither race nor color nor creed. It draws no fishing lines. If you have ever tried to describe the one that got away; if you have ever sought to explain how you lost all your tackle on the daddy of 'em all; if you have ever attempted to tiptoe home at night with an empty creel—a feat comparable to sneaking a ten-ton whale up Main Street—and have been hailed by some well-meaning acquaintance with the cheerful inquiry, "What luck?"; or jiggled a sulking trout with a horsehair snare; or patronized the inevitable small boy with willow pole and bent pin—if, in other words, you have ever fished at all, then you are automatically elected.

The rules and regulations for the club are few. Each session is usually conducted in a free-for-all style, with every angler for himself, catch-as-catch-can, weights unlimited, and no hoax barred. The symbols of brotherhood are the same in every fishing lodge from Montreal to Vancouver:

National Coat of Arms: a ten-pound rainbow rampant on a broken rod with crossed hearts, a Bible, and hand upraised.

National Insignia: an empty creel.

Secret Sign: holding both hands before the face from one to six feet apart (depending upon the individual's qualifications as a member of the club in good standing), shaking the head sadly, and murmuring: "No kidding, it was this big—"

Secret Passwords:

1. The water was too high.
2. The water was too low.
3. The stream was too muddy.
4. The stream was too clear.
5. The weather was too hot.
6. The weather was too cold.
7. The weather was unusual.

Universal Symbol of the Brotherhood: a worm.

There are no regular meetings of the Fish Liars' Club. They are held any time, any place, on the bank of a stream, in the Pullman smoker, in the parlor—wherever there are two or more fishermen gathered together. Sometimes even one fisherman can hold a meeting, provided he can find a non-fisherman to listen to him.

For example, as a self-appointed Field Secretary of the organization, I made a careful survey this past summer of some half-dozen of the famous fishing lakes that are dotted across Canada, strung like glassy beads along the tiny thread of the Canadian National Railroad from Montreal to Vancouver. In the course of my spectacular nonstop fishing flight from coast to coast, I worked the famous waters of Lake Nipigon for speckled trout, I tried for muskellunge and great northern pike in western Ontario, I fished for natives and Dolly Varden in Jasper Park in Alberta, for rainbow and mackinaw in Stuart Lake in British Columbia, for steelhead

trout and coho and tyee salmon on Vancouver Island, for grayling in
Alaska. Wherever I went, I found a local lodge of the Fish Liars' Club in
open and violent session.

Sometimes I couldn't even get a word in edgewise.

My first official meeting was held at Mud River Bridge in Ontario,
Lake Nipigon Chapter, Bill Bruce Lodge No. 1 in a pouring rain. For
forty days and forty nights that unseasonable spring, a steady downpour
had raised the waters of the Nipigon district from eight to ten feet above
normal. Lowlands were flooded, streams were torrents, the shallowest
riffles had become raging cataracts that were impossible to wade.
Campsites were half submerged under the yellow flood, only the tops of
benches and tables showing. Worst of all, the swollen rapids had concen-
trated great armies of suckers in the deep trout pools, and the sluggish
fish I took from that roily water were chockablock with sucker spawn and
oozed sago pudding when we squeezed them in our hand. In the face of
these conditions, a dry fly stood no more chance than an umbrella in a
hurricane.

I did not like to give up. Perhaps at the head of the White Sand River
the water would be down a little. For two days I struggled hopefully
upstream, chopping through the barriers of fallen spruce and tamarack,
shouldering against the heavy current, fighting the myriads of mosquitoes
that bred in swarms in the flooded marshland. They were all tied on
number twos, those Nipigon mosquitoes, and they hooked neatly with
every cast. In vain I smeared my face and hands with fly dope to keep
them off.

"It ain't no use," Frank concluded. "They just use the oil to keep their
drills from getting hot."

It began to look more encouraging as the stream narrowed toward its
source and the water grew less heavy and roily. Below a waterfall, the
stream formed a deep, quiet pool surrounded by birch and overhanging
spruce. Near the opposite bank, a submerged ledge or rock offered a natural pocket, fleeced with foam patches, a perfect lie for a fish; the current
of air generated by the waterfall obligingly formed a funnel that blew the
mosquitoes away from the pool. Here, if anywhere, there should be trout.
We linked arms and leaned our combined weight against the rush of
water as we waded cautiously across the stream, keeping our eyes fixed
on the eddy below the hidden boulder, and I made a short horizontal cast

toward the farther shore. The fly drifted temptingly for an instant over that black, silent eddy.

Nothing. I retrieved the line, stripped in a little, sent it backward through the air with a flick of the wrist, forward, backward again through the guides, then forward once more in a swift descending arc, the heavy tapered body of the line feeling its way accurately toward that spot under the overhanging spruce. I checked the cast exactly as it straightened, so that the light Cahill fluttered down like a leaf onto the stream. Once more it glided accurately under the spruce.

Abruptly the water swelled behind it. The fly disappeared. I lifted the tip of the rod slowly, tightened on it, struck. Instantly the rod doubled, the reel yelled, the line zigzagged and hummed against the current like the string of a violin. Downstream, across, up. Keep the line taut. Then the bottom of the stream turned over, and the fighting monster rolled once in a majestic swirl, thrashing his head from side to side like a bull-dog, disappearing again in a paralyzing glimpse of great green sides and shoulders turning, plunging, fighting toward whitewater.

I laid out my catch proudly that night. They were not heavy trout to be sure, and there were not many of them, but I had no complaints to make. I had wrested my fish in next-to-impossible conditions. Our camp had been the last word in comfort: Jack the cook had managed to solve a Russian puzzle of telescoping stovepipes and collapsible ovens to produce hot roast beef, chocolate layer cakes, and fresh doughnuts. In every way the trip had been a success, but....

"You ought to be here when conditions are right," said Bill, eyeing our catch a trifle coldly. "Six- and eight-pound trout are nothing, then. No mosquitoes. Wade every pool. They'll take a dry like nobody's business. Veritable fisherman's paradise." He sighed. "No, you really can't judge the Nipigon right now. The weather," he added, bringing down his gavel as the first meeting of the Fish Liars' Club adjourned, *"is unusual."*

*M*ike, of the Hudson, Ontario Chapter, called the second meeting of the Fish Liars' Club to order. "If you want muskies," he said, "we'll show you more muskies than you ever saw before. We got muskies here so big that you have to cut them in half before you photograph them so that people will believe you."

Cliff Lake is a short hour's hop by plane north of Hudson. We flew low under the threatening ceiling, banked over a green-blue fragment of jigsaw puzzle whose shores had been carved by an eccentric scroll saw into a maze of coves and inlets, and taxied down onto the rain-swept surface. Our weather still held: cold and gray and damp. We made dry camp in a welcome trapper's cabin while Mike rummaged through my duffel. He selected a reel from my tackle box, rigged it onto a light five-foot rod, pawed over my lures, and held up at last about a 5/0 hook, tied with a Red Ibis. "There's about your muskie outfit." As we shoved off a weedy shoal in the center of the lake, Shorty glanced at the gathering clouds.

"No good for muskie," he began, stopping the boat a moment to fill his pipe after we had trolled an hour without a strike. "Muskie go down when she starts to rain, won't come up till she starts to—"

We did not even know when it struck. My lure had sunk rather deep while the boat drifted, and the reel clicked once or twice so gently that I thought at first we were in a weed.

Shorty broke off, gazed at the taut line suspiciously, and began to back the boat. The line continued to got out very slowly, then more swiftly. I struck. It sounded immediately, fighting downward with short, savage tugs, and I gave it its head. Then, abruptly, it rose.

It charged the boat like a bull moose crashing through a thicket. I saw it for the first time as it came half out of water some sixty feet from the boat—a monster tiger muskie—swirling, lashing its tail furiously, kicking a shower of water behind it as it thrashed and plunged again. We pumped the rod and worked the reel desperately. For ten minutes, twenty minutes, half an hour, it fought as only a tiger muskie can—diving, boiling to the top again, floundering over and over, yanking its massive head backward. Once I saw the spinner, its barb set all too insecurely in a thin strip of gristle at the very corner of the mouth. My only chance was to keep that line taut, to be ready with the net when the fish was close. Forty minutes. The frantic runs were growing shorter. I held the net in readiness. It came up once more, opened its mouth wearily, and rolled once lazily over the line. I had a glimpse of great white jaws, a greenish blur in the water, and the sudden flash of the spinner loose in the air; and then the line went limp.

"And I bet it would have gone way over thirty pounds," Mike mourned, wringing his hands. "I know that shoal. I've seen 'em lying there forty and fifty pounds. I wouldn't be surprised if it'd even gone over fifty. I bet it would have gone sixty pounds or even seventy." He sighed, as the second meeting of the Fish Liars' Club drew to a pleasant close, *"if only it hadn't got away..."*

At least, the Jasper Park Chapter of the Fish Liars' Club can do nothing much to embellish the scenery—that is tops. For a million years, nature groaned and sweated to evolve this stupendous circus of mountains and sheer ridges, high, gleaming glaciers, and icy torrents that wind in silver ribbons down the precipices into the valleys.

I had never cast a fly in more beautiful surroundings. I fished Beaver Lake, an expanse of flooded muskeg that boiled with one-pound trout like a hatchery at feeding time and offered a fighting native for every barbless Fawning Cahill that I laid upon its placid surface.

We left the cushioned ease of the lodge and moved north by car. My guide was a big-game hunter, sportsman, and outfitter in charge of horses and camping equipment in Jasper Park. We packed by saddle from Jasper Lodge to the connected ponds of Buffalo Prairie and worked for rainbow in the windy Valley of the Lakes. From there we went by horse, then canoe, and finally foot to Medicine Lake along the course of the rushing Maligne River (now and then try a tempting pool along the trail), on to the unparalleled grandeur of Maligne Lake, a nine-mile stretch of cold glacial water six thousand feet in the air ringed by lofty snow-capped peaks, the climax of the whole unbelievable show.

From Fort St. James, forty miles north of Vanderhoof on the Canadian National Railway, there extend some two hundred miles of connected lakes and streams, all of them navigable by launch, offering perhaps the largest continuous stretch of rainbow-trout waters in North America.

The trout were plentiful in the rivers, but I took nothing over three pounds; it was in the lakes that we would find those famous ten- and fifteen-pounders, the daddies of 'em all. We trolled Stuart Lake, Takla, and

Trembleur. I took rainbow up to ten pounds; reluctantly we turned the nose of the *Doris* toward Douglas Lodge at last, ready to meet the Pacific-Alaska plane that would swoop us up from Stuart Lake the following morning and take us to Alaska.

"Ain't really no use trying beyond here, anyways," said George, my guide, scowling at a craggy landmark on the shore of Trembleur Lake. "You might as well reel in now. I never heard of anybody taking one past this point."

And then it struck. I was reeling in as it hit the spoon, and it hooked itself solidly and kept going. It ran out a hundred, a hundred and fifty, two hundred feet of line in that first mad rush. The backing was beginning to run low; the spindle of the reel grew dangerously bare. In vain, George reversed the motor of the launch. There was no stopping that rampaging maniac. You might as well have lassoed the smokestack of the Twentieth Century. I held the howling reel, and watching the flying handle helplessly, shut my eyes.

It jumped twelve times in those next agonizing twenty minutes; it rushed and plunged; it tried all the tricks that a fighting rainbow knows. The leader still held, the line never slackened, the tip of the rod met each erratic plunge with a stiff upward jerk. It came to the boat at last, floundering half-drowned in the water, and George hauled it on board. He mopped his brow and gazed in silence at the indicator of the scales teetering between twelve and thirteen pounds under the limp weight of that silver-sided beauty.

"You know," he murmured at last, "that fish really should have gone more than twelve-and-a-half pounds."

I admired the rainbow hopefully.

"Yes sir, now you know," added George, thereby founding on the spot the Stuart Lake Chapter of the Fish Liars' Club, Douglas Lodge No. 333, *"that fish would of gone fifteen pounds if it hadn't just spawned."*

"*L*ooka there, boys," George said, striding excitedly up and down the Chamber of Commerce offices in Victoria. "You wanna see what a tyee salmon really looks like?" He paused and gestured proudly toward a framed picture hanging on the wall. "How much do you think that one'd weigh? Fifty-three pounds," he added hurriedly, to prevent the possibility of our belittling his fish by too modest a guess.

I gazed at the photograph in patent admiration. Even in juxtaposition with the triumphant figure of George, himself a specimen of no mean proportions, the silhouette of that monster salmon, dangling from the official scales of the Tyee Club of British Columbia, was an awe-inspiring sight. George beamed.

"See what they give you if you land a fish like that? See what you get for taking a tyee over fifty pounds? Looka there, boys." He placed a thumb behind his lapel and thrust forward a shiny good emblem. "Been fishing the Campbell River every season for ten years to get that button. Official award of the Tyee Club of British Columbia. How'd you like a gold button like that?"

I sighed enviously.

"Campbell River's about the only spot you can take these big Pacific salmon on light tackle," Mr. Warren explained. "Members come here to Vancouver Island from Australia and Scotland and China every year to fish this late August run. Anybody who gets a salmon over thirty pounds is eligible to join the club. Got to follow the Tyee regulations, of course," he explained, tossing me a 1934 rule book. "Rod at least six feet in length, six-ounce bamboo tip, not more than twenty-five-pound test line, single hook, handle your fish alone, without help from the guide." He rubbed his hands briskly. "Well, the car's all set. Hundred-mile drive ahead. Hit the hay early. Got to get up at four a.m. to catch the tide. Let's get going. Of course you won't land a gold-button fish like mine every day of the week," he added, casting a last affectionate glance over his shoulder at the photograph on the wall. They've only taken a dozen that size in the Tyee Club's history. But there's always the chance of a bronze button over thirty pounds, or even a silver over forty. At least it's worth a try."

We moved out into the black silence of Discovery Passage and headed down the channel toward the salmon grounds just off the mouth of the Campbell River. Occasionally we passed other dim shapes, members of the early morning fleet that had already started trolling with the slackening tide, the clunk of oars in metal locks sounding hollowly over the water. In the strange silence of dawn, the explosive smash of a playful salmon leaping just aft of our boat brought me half erect with an involuntary gasp. I reached eagerly for the rod and dangling metal lure.

"Don't touch that spoon!" cried Old Man Smith, my guide on this leg of the trip. He glared with some alarm. He fondled the spoon soothingly, stroking its concave sides gently with a chamois rag. "Your fingers will tarnish the silver if they touch it. I made this spoon myself and it's never failed to take a trophy tyee each season. I'd rather lose my right arm than have anything happen to this spoon." He handed me the rod. "All right, now you can let it out."

I began to pay out the line nervously, watching for the white mark that would indicate when we had reached the club's maximum trolling length of sixty feet. I felt a trifle crushed. Behind us, Old Man Smith rowed in loaded silence; I could feel his resentful eyes fixed on the back of my neck. I checked the reel, elevated the rod to the proper angle, and stared at the other boats moving back and forth slowly across the quiet inlet, gradually grown pearl-grey and pink in the increasing dawn.

"Was that a strike?" asked Old Man Smith suddenly.

I turned and gazed at him in bewilderment.

"Don't look at me; watch the tip of your rod," he said impatiently. "You can tell if the spoon is working right by the action of the tip."

I stared dutifully at the tip nodding steadily like a palsied octogenarian as the swiveled spoon turned underwater. Abruptly I saw it dip a little lower and felt simultaneously a faint tug on the line. I struck. Something began to move away very gently, its slight pull almost imperceptible against the motion of the boat. The bottom, of course. I began to reel in the line.

"Take care," said Old Man Smith with some uncanny instinct that I have never understood. "You're into a big one there."

I smiled tolerantly as I continued to take in line. No fish of any size would come to us so casually as this. I glanced at my wristwatch—5:10. I had not yet been out fifteen minutes. It was all too easy. I sighed as I led our unseen captive steadily to the boat without a struggle. So this was the famed tyee fishing! Old Man Smith rose and poised his gaff. I lifted the rod, saw the great head of a salmon rise to the surface beside me and then, as my heart skipped a beat, I saw a black, spade-like tail cut the water five incredible feet away.

"My Lord," Old Man Smith whispered faintly, "it's over fifty pounds!"

The tyee saw us at the same instant; saw us, turned, and ran. I do not know how far he ran. I do not recall distinctly what happened in the crowded hour that elapsed before we saw him on the surface again. I worked the reel desperately, taking in what line I dared, giving him his head when he chose to sound, burying the butt of the rod into the pit of my stomach, tugging, fighting, praying.

Abruptly, the maddened salmon turned and charged directly through the center of the fishing fleet like a runaway horse, scattering indignant boats right and left, towing us helplessly in his wake. He carried us into the middle of the channel, back toward the treacherous weed-lined shore, over the bars, and out at last toward deep water again. The dawn had broken, and in the misty light we saw him clearly for the first time as he swirled to the top a hundred yards away—majestic, terrifying, huge beyond belief.

The salmon had halted again. My tired fingers tried to turn the reel handle in vain. It was too much. I couldn't make it. I could scarcely hold the rod. My hands shook, I had no strength left in wrist or arm. He was sulking now, tugging the line with quick, impatient jolts that sent throbs of pain up my numbed arm to my shoulder. I glanced at the shaking dial of my watch—6:20. The perspiration was running into my eyes. The rod twisted perilously in my damp hands. I could no longer close my fingers tight against the butt. I heard Old Man Smith's voice at last: "I think he's coming in now."

He came inch by inch, in a proud death march, fighting to the finish. He wallowed and rolled feebly, sank out of sight in a final desperate plunge, rose, and swirled again. Now we could see his silvery sides turning over weakly in spite of the powerful sweeps of that thrashing tail. He was not swimming now. We dragged him nearer the waiting gaff. He rolled once more and lay helpless on his side. The moment was at hand. The gaff descended, missed in its haste, and caught a mere strip of skin in the top of his head. In the nick of time, Old Man Smith hooked a hand under the gills, gave a mighty heave, and hauled him over the side into the boat. He flopped once and lay still. We weighed him in at 6:30, just an hour and a half from the time we had left Painter's Landing. On the official scales of the Tyee Club, he went exactly fifty-five pounds. We laid him on the bench, cleaned the patches of black scum still caked to his sides, and then covered him with coarse sand. We went solemnly to tell George.

It was a gloomy meeting of the Fish Liars' Club, Campbell River Local No. 1001, which was held on that strip of beach a couple of hours later. While the cameras were being assembled, we unearthed our fish and dusted the sand from his gleaming sides. George shook his head hopelessly. For once the Fish Liars' Club could find nothing to say. There were no alibis left. The impossible had happened. The salmon weighed fifty-five pounds. It was a gold-button fish. It had been hooked during the first ten minutes that we had ever fished for tyee. It was the only fish hooked that morning; the last heavy fish, we subsequently learned, that was taken that year. It had been taken legally, according to the Tyee Club rules. Our tackle had not broken. The fish hadn't just spawned. Even the weather had been usual. George faced his fellow members with a doleful expression.

"Well, anyway," he said, "you can't say this isn't a fisher-man's paradise."

With heavy hearts the members of the Fish Liars' Club lifted the salmon and hung it on the scales. We did not notice that its mouth was still clogged with sand. The cameras were poised in readiness. We happened to glance at the figures on the scales.

The salmon weighed fifty-six pounds.

We looked at each other in silence. George turned his head away tactfully. Very solemnly, I took my worn membership card from the band of my hat and placed it in the salmon's gaping mouth.

It is with deep regret that I have tendered my resignation to the Fish Liars' Club of Fairbanks, Alaska. I feel that I am not worthy of the honor after all. I resign in favor of that fish.

Seventeen

Rules of the Club

I should put my fly directly behind that boulder. There the current spends its force and parts on either side in a rippling, satin flow; and there in the dead backwater above the rock, the yellow-white foam from the tumbling water circles aimlessly for a moment before it is snatched downstream. I should strip the line a little; send it backward with a flick of the wrist and then forward, and backward, and then singing forward suddenly through the agate eyes, feeling its way like a snake, wandering a little and wavering as it writhes down and rests fly-first upon the creamy froth, rides lightly for a moment, turns slowly with the endless circle of the eddy, and then darts off the pillow of foam and hurtles downstream after the dragging line...

Late May, perhaps, or June; and it would be that hour of the afternoon when the blue smoke rises off the meadows, and the bark of a dog and distinct tinkle of cattle are strangely near in the hollow silence. The cooling air carries every odor sharply: the dank body-smell of a pasture still steaming from the recent sun, manure turned into a freshly plowed field, wood-smoke, and the acid smell of hickory. The stream is running down after a recent rain and chuckles and slaps at the white cobbles along the shore; the long, flat riffles that we fished during the hot afternoon are humming below us.

Here the stretch of stream is deeper, widening in a smooth fan from the boulder at the lip of the flat. The current glides silently along the left bank, under the overhanging willows and alders. A bluish-grey midge comes bouncing and spanking downstream, flapping its wings helplessly in the air, dropping back on its tail and skidding merrily with the current; under a small willow, the water parts with a suck and a noiseless swirl, and when the surface flattens again, the midge is gone. Mark the place— under that small willow.

A scoop of the hand would capture another midge as it flutters by on the surface; and with it locked between thumb and forefinger, I should sink back on a white, round rock at the side of the stream with the water flattening the rubber of my boots cool against my leg and study the insect. Bluish-grey wings. A bit of yellow on the tail. Well, out with the fly box and pick over the assortment of hand-tied flies critically. Cahill, Hare's Ear; say, a Whirling Dun, starling's feathers for wings, a wrapping of mole's fur around the body, and the legs and tail of ginger hackle. A reasonable imitation of the midge in my fingers. A light brush of mucelin to make it float; tie it on the silvery leader and swing it into the air. The reel snarls as it unwinds; the line travels forward, backward, suddenly forward again in a horizontal cast across the flat water to the gliding current along the left bank. The fly rides like a speck of light downstream past the small willow.

Does a small hump of water follow it for a moment and then disappear? A flick of the wrist retrieves the fly into the air before it drowns; another flick lays it gently a foot above the willow, and it glides down again into the shadows. The water parts; the bottom of the stream turns over suddenly, and the line hums taut in a blurred fan of rainbow drops, singing against the current like the string of a cello, cutting upstream at an angle, slicing a half-circle mid-current, suddenly slackening, following the invisible fighting captive as he darts about below the surface or breaks at last in a flash of whitewater, the glimpse of a greenish shoulder and a white belly plunging down...

Your Cabots of Back Bay may have their little clique; your Pomeranian may glance condescendingly through his limousine window at the mongrel in the gutter; your patent cigar-lighter may look down on a book of matches. But nowhere is there a snobbery quite so complete as the snobbery of the dry fly fisherman. The wet fly fisherman is unenlightened; the worm fisherman is anathema; the man who does not fish at all—but they are not men who do not fish at all. Two-legged, pale, soulless creatures, perhaps, who see the first Saturday in April come and go, who count off May and early June as just one more step toward the hot weather; who pass by a tackle store window without a longing stab and lingering, hungry eyes; who drive over a rumbling bridge without a swift, speculative glance at the pools and eddies in the stream below; who could read this story without murmuring indignantly: "This guy doesn't know what he's talking about. In the first place, a Whirling Dun isn't..." They are mice, not men.

There is a strange, haunted look in the true angler's eye as the Opening Day draws nearer. They stroll along Madison Avenue with a curious plodding motion, as though they were wading upstream against an imaginary current. They handle their umbrellas tenderly, playing them unconsciously in the air with a reminiscent flick of the wrist and pointing them at a choice eddy in the stream of traffic. In their offices, they stand dreamily by the hour while telephones ring and papers pile high, turning the pencil sharpener slowly as they wind a distant reel.

Their bedroom lights burn late into the night that first week in April, as they sort over their tackle, soak their leaders, test their lines, toil over their flies, fit together their rods, and play them once or twice cautiously in the narrow space between bedpost and bureau, handling them with all the reverence of an old pair of dueling pistols.

Of an afternoon, perhaps, they congregate over the camphor-soaked trays at Abercrombie & Fitch, gesturing, talking in a hushed monotone, picking over the Downey flies critically, examining the expensive Hardy reels, purchasing at last one small gut leader and discussing the latest bulletins from the Front: "Say, there's pretty much snow up there still," "Hear the Beaverkill's very high," "This time last year..."

It is an exacting order. Its membership is exclusive; its initiation is long and slow; its brethren of the angle, upon joining, are pledged to the solemn conviction that anyone who is not a dry fly fisherman is simply not quite bright. And the opportunities for an innocent novice who entertains the bland assumption that the purpose of fishing is merely to catch fish, and that it all has something to do somehow with lowering a piece of pork over the side of a boat on a hot afternoon on Long Island Sound—the opportunities for such a novice to augment this preconceived conviction of the dry fly fisherman are staggering. The very terminology of the tackle offers innumerable pitfalls to a well-meaning layman.

For example, at the cost of alienating the sensitive angler for life, never refer to his rod as a "pole." Never call his line a "string." Never call his trout flies "them little things," nor inquire genially if his wife knitted them for him. Never ask if the trout are apt to go for him when he's in the water. Never attempt to open conversation with him by remarking in an amiable tone, "You know, I used to be sort of a fisherman myself. I used to be quite fond of diggin' clams. Yep," while clasping the hands behind the back and nodding companionably, "There's quite an art in diggin' clams right. You have to know how to feel for them with your toe and..." And never, above all else, greet a weary angler who is sneaking guiltily toward home with his creel bouncing all too lightly on his hip with the well-meaning hail, "Hi! Catch anything?"

These are the things that draw dry fly fishermen closer together; these, and the three great Common Prejudices that bind them with bands of steel in a vast brotherhood: Contempt for the Fish Hog, Contempt for all Lady Anglers, and Contempt for Fishermen Who Use Worms.

Fish Hogs should be, by all logic, beneath contempt. Their breed should be exterminated with no more consideration than is afforded the black fly on your neck. They bully their way downstream—you never see them fishing dry—wallowing into the choicest eddies, rooting their snouts along the deep banks, doing valiant battle with a six-inch trout—legal prey under a criminal law that permits the capture of these immature fish—and limiting the number of their catch only to the capacity of their pockets, so that they may count their noble total at the end of the day and enter it in some imaginary competition for Biggest Catch. Their standard of success depends entirely on the number of fish in their basket, not the expert handling of their rod nor their canny imitation of the natural fly on the water; not the battle of wits with the fighting trout; not even the sunshine and the clean air. They brag happily: "Sure, I bet Joe I'd get a hun'erd and fifty this week.... Eat them? Me? No, fish make me sick. No, I'll have to just give them to the cat..." And the curious irony is the luck that invariably attends them. Trout that ignore a true sportsman will fairly leap into the bulging creel of the Fish Hog. No wonder I get so sore.

My dislike for Lady Anglers may have sprung from an old prejudice that has run in the Ford family for generations against women in bloomers. I come from an old New England stock that believes firmly that women do not belong in pants; and a glance at stenographers hiking along the Palisades on Sunday in ballooning slacks, silk stockings, and high heels has gone a long way toward developing a general phobia of female fishermen, female big-game hunters, female explorers, and female cowboys.

I do not deny that women have their place, but I would fight to the death for a national ordinance proclaiming that their place is not on a trout stream. There they chatter, they giggle, they splash and flounder into the choicest pools, they slap mosquitoes, they complain, they powder their noses at the instant they are landing their biggest fish. They bicker and quarrel and lose their tempers, they tangle their lines in overhanging balsams and I have to climb up for them; they drop their leader boxes into deep pools, and I have to dive down for them. They catch their hooks in embarrassing parts of their anatomy, and I have to crawl on my hands and knees into the bushes and hide my eyes like a gentleman. I am an acknowledged idealist about women and an admirer of the sex, but I serve them fair notice: On a trout stream, they are not at their best.

And as for Worm Fishermen...

Last summer our President put a worm on a hook and caught a nice fish and subsequently posed with it before the cameras wearing a trim business suit and starched collar while the First Lady held two white collies on a leash and smiled approvingly at her husband's skill. And immediately the hue and cry went around the land that worm fishing was the most successful method of catching trout.

So it is. No fly fisherman will dispute the point.

You can catch more trout with worms than with any other device, except possibly dynamite. Similarly, you can transport a baseball more successfully to home plate by carrying it in your hip pocket, and a golf ball may be dropped into the winning hole with far greater ease if, instead of using a tiny stick with a metal knob on the end, you employ a broom and a shovel. The issue is entirely one of sportsmanship.

I do not blame our President. After all, it was not so long ago that he came out in print against any form of fishing whatsoever. His progress is slow, but encouraging. If he finds pleasure now in angling with a worm, that is very nice indeed, and no one is happier than I to see him get some fresh air and put a little color in those cheeks. Perhaps after he has relinquished the Presidency and its attendant worries, he may be able to devote a little more time to his angling and eventually—who knows?—develop into a first-class dry fly fisherman. I do hope, however, that next time he will take off that starched collar. It only scares the fish.

The attitude of the dry fly fisherman toward the fisherman who uses a worm is a little tolerant and sympathetic. In all probability, he was a worm fisherman once himself. Perhaps he also worked his way from the cane pole to the sunk fly, and from the sunk fly he progressed at last to the fine art of the dry fly and the split bamboo. There are hopes for these other fellows. After all, they have the stuff in them. And someday they, too, may know that ecstatic instant of a midge well-imitated, a cast well-made, the plunging strike and screaming reel, and the lashing, rearing captive, turning in mid-air in a comet's tail of silver spray, burning the line upstream, fighting, fighting toward whitewater...

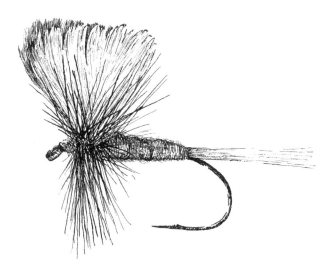

Eighteen

Rainbows in the Chilean Sky

The lake was at ten thousand feet, the nearest I have ever fished to heaven. We had smeared our faces like striped Indians with white ointment borrowed from an Air Force survival kit; at this altitude, the sun burns with a fierce heat that sears the skin. Nothing was quite real, here at the top of the Andes, the highest range in the Western world.

The smoke from an active volcano made a purple smudge across the icy peaks surrounding the lake, and ahead of us, a flock of pink flamingos—as unreal as a dream—rose and wheeled in exotic flight past a patch of fresh-fallen snow.

But the fishing was the most unreal of all. There were three of us in the boat, casting toward the high, serrated cliff along the shore. Between the weed bed and the base of the cliff was a stretch of clear water, and that was where the big ones lay. We threw our lures in unison. Simultaneously we had three hits; three rods lifted; three lines tightened. Three fish came out of water at the same moment—rainbows weighing an average of ten pounds each—the three heaviest trout I have ever seen in the air at once. Too late, Dan raced ashore for his camera.

"Relax," we consoled him. "It wouldn't do any good to take a picture. Nobody'd believe it anyway..."

I couldn't believe it myself, and I'd seen a lot of fishing. But I'd never seen Chile. I'd heard about the fabled trout of the Andes, of course, rainbows transplanted originally from the United States to Germany, and then brought all the way from Germany to South America, grown to prodigious size in these food-packed Chilean streams. Nobody could say how big, nobody had any photographs, nobody knew for sure. That was why I went five thousand miles to fish the waters of Chile.

But how could I write about what I saw and make it sound true? Rivers whose rapids and eddies literally roll with trout, where an evening hatch of insects may produce a dozen good fish rising at once within the cast of a rod. Lakes set at the base of snow-capped volcanoes where salmon and sea-run rainbow cruise in the crystal waters. The Rio Tolten, Chile's best known trout stream, where perspiring boatmen row backward all day against the current as the angler drifts luxuriously downstream, casting ahead into the deep, dark holes. The Rio Quesapu, where we took acrobatic browns up to six pounds on a dry fly. Lake Maule, where we caught and released not less than a hundred rainbow trout between eight and ten pounds—any one would have been the trout of a lifetime back in the States—in a couple of unbelievable afternoons.

Here is the other half of the sportsman's year. March is autumn down here, because this is below the equator, and everything is backward. Winter is summer, you can't eat oysters in a month with "R" in it, and the water in the bathtub swirls counterclockwise as it flows out of the drain, your shadow moves in the opposite direction—from left to right (or is it from right to left?)— people say goodbye when they meet you on the street, and the clocks go *tock-tick*.

From November to April, when trout fishing is closed everywhere in the States and the streams are locked with ice, the season in South America is at its height. Chile is the answer to an angler's prayer. Now he can keep right on fishing the whole year round.

*C*hile is the southwestern coastline of South America, and very little else. It is the sliver of land between the Andes and the Pacific, a thousand miles long and no more than two hundred miles across at its widest point. Santiago lies due south of New York, and you can get there in less than twenty-four hours. You leave Miami at night via Panagra—the Pan American Grace Airways that services Chile—and touch Panama at midnight, Lima at breakfast time, Santiago for lunch. That's about the same as a flight to California. And you travel in such luxury as you've never known aloft: crisp martinis before dinner, Argentine beef, fine Chilean wines. You can relax in the comfortable Fiesta Lounge, or sleep in beds if you prefer, or if you're a fisherman, you can talk rising trout all night with the pilot. These Panagra fliers, like most flying people I know, can place a fly on the water as easily as they set down their big four-engined airplanes. The captain of the plane I was on was no exception. I attended eagerly as he put his controls on automatic, got out a pencil, and marked the best places on a map of Chile. "Let's begin at the bottom. Down here below Osorno is the Lakes Country, and here about halfway is the Tolten River, and up here—" he put a dot on the map "— is Lake Maule. One of our boys got an eigh-teen-pounder out of Maule on his last layover. If I were you, I'd hit the south part first. It's getting pretty late in the year down there..."

So we planned to start with the Lakes Country, at the extreme south of Chile, before winter arrived with April. Already we'd heard in Santiago that the weather at Osorno was closing in. Our chartered single-engine plane took off from Santiago in flawless sunshine, and the first hour of the flight south was spectacularly beautiful. The sea was to our right; beneath us lay the checkerboard of flat, fertile vineyards that produce some of the world's finest wines, and to our left, the majestic Andes marched against the sky. One disgruntled Ande, just over the Argentine border, gave off three successive puffs of black volcanic smoke as we passed; they blended together to form a mushroom-shaped cloud. "Peron's bomb," the pilot chuckled. He explained that last month a local airlines pilot had witnessed the same phenomenon and had reported excitedly that Peron was setting off an atomic explosion.

We crossed a ribbon of river, winding down from the mountains; our map said this was the Maule, and somewhere to the westward would be the fabulous lake that was its source. Half an hour later we passed over another lake, with a small settlement on its near shore. "Villarrica," the pilot said. He dipped a wing to show us the river flowing out of the lake through a deep gorge, dotted with white rapids. "That's the Tolten."

The weather was growing increasingly sour; a bank of clouds moved toward us out of the south, blanketing the ground, and the wind began to buffet the plane. We bounced and banged and sideslipped while the pilot wrestled the controls, fighting to make Osorno. Each minute it grew worse; the plane veered and fishtailed, dropped a couple of hundred feet, and rode up again like a homesick angel. We clenched our teeth to keep them from chipping. A storm in the Andes is nothing to fool with. We did a one-eighty too soon, and bucked back north through solid soup. Clouds were everywhere, and some of those clouds had rocks in them. The pilot wiped perspiration from his forehead and watched the gas indi-cator. At last he found a hole in the stuff and spiraled down through it, and we saw Villarrica below us, grey with rain. We made two low passes over the town to signal for transportation, lowered our wheels, and landed on a cow pasture, braking to a halt on the slippery grass in front of a herd of startled Holsteins. We taxied back across the meadow to an ancient barn with silo that served as municipal airport and hangar for visiting aircraft. Right then, I wouldn't have swapped it for La Guardia.

A battered native taxicab picked us up and took us to Villarrica's only hostelry, which had the somewhat improbable name of "Hotel Yachting Club." Maybe it was our recent unnerving experience—maybe it was the double Scotch I ordered on arrival—but it seemed to me that the Hotel Yachting Club was the most comfortable inn I'd ever seen. We dried in front of the fire; we had a fine dinner with wine; we began making plans to fish the famous Tolten as soon as the rain stopped. Our host, as efficient as he was courteous, assured us that he would arrange the boatmen for tomorrow. How was the fishing? He sighed. He would be perfectly frank with us: The fishing was, how would you say, not so good, eh? But tomorrow we would see for ourselves.

Tomorrow we saw. The sun came out after breakfast, and we set out in two flat-bottomed rowboats, heading down the lake to the river's mouth. We could hear the thunder of the rapids as we approached. The outlet of the lake was a narrow gorge through which the water poured in a series of whirlpools and treacherous eddies, studded with sharp, protruding ledges against which the river flung its full force. To my surprise, the boatman drifted bow-first unconcernedly into the very center of this maelstrom, then dug in his oars and began to row frantically upstream, at the same time signaling me to start casting.

I threw out the fly a little uncertainly, and it was instantly sucked out of sight. For a moment the boatman seemed to be winning his battle with the current and we hung there tenuously in the boiling water while I cast again. Then he started thrashing with the oars for all he was worth, and we slithered diagonally across stream and halted once more, just above the jagged boulder. I laid the fly beside the rock and promptly had a strike. In that heavy water, it felt like the daddy of them all. The boatman lifted his oars, our bow missed the boulder by inches as we catapulted downstream past it, and we chased the fish into quieter water. I lifted it over the side. It was about eight inches.

I cast again and again while the boatman fought the current, and we zigzagged back and forth across the river. He would drift to the very brink of a rapids, paddle for dear life to keep from being swept over, then whirl downstream toward another fast eddy. At last I was beginning to get the idea. The boatman was doing the fishing. He was placing the fly wherever he wished by maneuvering the boat, and my abortive efforts to cast were only making things harder for him. After that I relaxed, letting the fly trail below me, and watched him work.

He worked skillfully, lowering the lure into a likely pocket, allowing it to dangle there for a moment, then rowing diagonally across the stream, dragging the fly with him. The erratic motion of the boat gave the fly a lifelike action in the water. He seemed to know his river, making for a particular hole that he knew, entirely passing up other stretches I would have thought more promising. Sometimes he would quit and hoist both oars out of water, and we would go screaming down through the rapids, bobbing like a cork, for half a mile or more.

The only trouble was that we didn't get any fish. Once or twice I persuaded him to let me out on a gravel bar so I could stand and cast; I managed to pick up a couple of trout that way. The rest of the time, I leaned back contentedly and watched the scenery whirl by. The scenery alone was worth the trip. The high banks were covered with the enormous spiny leaves of the *palca*, some of them four or five feet across; the bell-shaped flowers of the *copihue*, the national flower of Chile, hung overhead in graceful clusters, and fuchsia bushes in full bloom leaned out over the water, shedding their red and purple blossoms onto the current. White-faced rapids ducks peeked at us from behind the rocks, and a sociable family of white egrets moved downstream with us, flapping from tree to tree. Now and then the meandering river would make a complete turn, and we would be looking back at the distant white cone of Villarrica Volcano, turning pink with the setting sun. We halted at dusk, some twenty miles downstream, delivered our boats to a waiting team of oxen that would haul them back to town that night, and returned to the Hotel Yachting Club in our faithful battered taxicab. Our host met us at the door with a sad smile.

"You see?" he said resignedly.

I suspect that our lack of success on the Toltan was due, in part at least, to the overabundance of bottom feed—the fish we opened were glutted with small crawfish and snails—and the almost total lack of any insect life on the surface. The Rio Quesapu, to which we progressed as soon as the weather cleared in the south, was just the other way around. Here the underwater feed was no more than normal, and the insect hatches at dusk reminded me of the old days on the Beaverkill.

The Quesapu is a wide, deep, rowdy stream with thundering cataracts and flat, foaming pools below them, with rapids and eddies and long, fast runs, with black potholes beneath the ledges where the water is almost still and you can see the big rainbow and salmon finning. The shore is bare, strewn with big boulders, and you can cast anywhere. It is one of the most beautiful fly fishing streams in the world.

The big hatches would occur about seven o'clock at night, just as the light was fading. We would station ourselves at strategic spots along the big river, or on the bank of an ice-cold feeder brook, as quiet and clear as an English chalk-stream, where the trout were so wary you had to use an extra tippet on your leader and a number fourteen or sixteen fly.

But it was in the main current that the big ones lay. We would stand and wait, watching the bumpy surface of the water, while the insects appeared out of nowhere and began to beat upstream, pelting our faces like wet snowflakes in an increasing swarm.

Ten yards in front of me, a little wave rose and fell regularly. I looked more closely; it was a trout rolling. All around me in the gathering dusk, other fish were surfacing to grab the insects as fast as they lit. I cast to a rise; there was a hungry swirl; I struck too fast, and yanked the fly out of its jaws. It was hard to set the barb in that fast water. I cast again, and was into a heavy brown that straightened out the hook before I brought him to the net. I fumbled to change flies in the darkness, holding fly and leader aloft to silhouette them against the last light in the sky while the feeding trout splashed and *clunked* around me, occasionally leaping clear out of the water and belly-whopping at my feet with a joyful smack.

That night the snow-capped peak of Osorno Volcano glowed like cold fire in the moonlight. The next day the peak was obscured by clouds. We did not see it again. The wind rose to a gale, and grey sheets of rain moved toward us across the base of the mountain. I never saw it rain harder. One afternoon we cast from the pier, three feet above the surface of the lake; the following morning the same pier was five feet underwater. Overnight that twenty-five mile lake had risen a total of eight feet, turning our lovely trout stream into a roily flood, submerging the road to

Osorno, and marooning us for three days. At last they sent an amphibian to fetch us out; we transferred to private plane and took off in a churning sea of mud and flew back to Santiago.

We fished the Maule with Major Fred and Captain Jerry—both highly decorated World War II fliers, and both ardent anglers. They were attached to the USAF Mission in Chile that serves as technical adviser to the Chilean Air Force. As a footloose Air Force colonel from the States, I had dropped by to pay my respects to my brother officers at the Mission, and somehow or other the conversation got around to fishing—take a group of Air Force people anywhere in the world, I've found, and sooner or later the conversation will get around to fishing. I've often wondered why so many fliers are natural fly fishermen. Maybe the same reflexes that go into piloting an airplane, the same instinctive rhythm and sense of timing, enable a man to handle a rod and cast a line and place a fly with precision. Fred and Jerry were particularly disturbed that I hadn't taken any really heavy trout in Chile. They would like to show me a certain little lake they knew about on their forthcoming weekend leave—a lake called the Maule.

It is an all-day drive from Santiago to the Maule, and the last half of the ride is hairy indeed. You climb straight up a narrow dirt trail scratched out of the side of the mountain, occasionally feeling your way around a fallen boulder or tilting perilously across a fresh slide of gravel that blocks the way. Below you, a drop of a sheer half-mile, the Maule River tumbles in a series of cascades, making a faint, steady thunder. The road is just wide enough for one car; if you meet an oncoming vehicle, you inch out onto the loose rubble until your rear wheel dangles over space, and the other car hugs the cliff as it scrapes past you. It is dangerous to drive after nightfall; we halted at dark, rolled up in sleeping bags on the side of the precipice, and waited for morning.

Daylight revealed a strange alpine world. We had climbed above timberline, and the slopes were covered with dwarfed shrubs and red, azalea-like flowers. A covey of mountain quail scurried uphill away from the car, flocks of pearl-breasted doves sideslipped back and forth across the road, and once we had to halt to let a flock of sheep go by, herded by a pair of shouting *huasos* in flat black hats and bright-colored *mantas*. All around us was an infinite angry ocean of white peaks; the eccentric cone of the Bell Tower rose high above the rest, and in the distance, beyond the flattened crater of the Little Beheaded, Peron's bomb sent up another mushroom cloud. A final hour's climb brought us to the summit, and Lake Maule lay cupped in the center of a wide, bare plateau, flat against the sky.

*T*here's always a wind at the top of the world, and the lake was covered with whitecaps when we arrived. We bailed out a leaky rowboat that we found chained to a rock, attached an outboard motor Fred had thoughtfully brought along, and set out for the line of cliffs on the far right side. Flocks of wild ducks huddled in the shelter of the coves; ahead of us a band of geese, magnified by the bright light, appeared as big as cattle as they waddled across a sandpit, looking back at us indignantly. In the middle of the lake there was quite a sea running. Big rollers broke over our bow, the air was filled with flying spray, and we were drenched to the skin by the time we made the other shore.

It was useless to attempt a fly in that wind; Fred and Jerry set up their spinning rods, and Dan and I resorted to throwing sticks and metal spoons. A weed bed lay about a hundred feet offshore, the tip of the grass just showing above the water, affording a natural source of food as well as protection for the big trout. Fred drew first blood. His initial cast was grabbed by a waiting trout, and his line sang like a high-tension wire as the fish raced for the weeds. Fred managed to check its rush, fought it through a series of spectacular leaps, and brought it alongside the boat. He looked down at the huge rainbow, wallowing in the water.

"Female," he said briefly. He gripped her behind the gills, held her underwater as he worked the barb out of her jaw, and released it with a little shove. I wondered what sportsman in the States would casually turn loose a ten-pound rainbow trout.

Dan followed with an eight-pound male that had swallowed the barb so deeply that it had to be killed. Jerry took a nice ten-pounder right after it. I nearly caught the heaviest one of the day when I made an abortive cast into the wind and my spoon whacked Jerry neatly behind an ear. If he hadn't gotten away, he'd have gone a hundred and sixty pounds.

Thereafter we split the boatload up, and some of us worked from shore. Dan rigged his fly rod and worked his way out to the end of a point of rocks where he had spotted a big one rising. Dan is the finest fly caster I have ever seen, but throwing a feather into the teeth of that gale was a supreme challenge. Dan laid the fly over the exact spot a dozen times without a miss until the rainbow could resist it no longer.

Suddenly Dan yelled, his reel screamed, the lake erupted, and a pink-sided monster catapulted into the air as though it were shot out of a cannon. It took Dan twenty minutes on that light tackle, but he led it to his feet at last and, with a final triumphant gesture, lifted it out of the water by the gills and held it aloft, wriggling in the air. It went nine-and-a-half pounds, a handsome trophy on a fly.

We took them on spoons; we took them on streamers; we took them singly and in pairs and, on several different occasions, three at a time. I have no idea how many trophy trout we actually turned loose that day and the next. We tried to figure it out as we boarded the big Panagra stra-to-liner to fly home, but we could not believe it ourselves. The Andes flattened and fell away behind us; by this time tomorrow, we would be back in the States. Lunch in Santiago one day, lunching in New York the next. Somehow, that was the hardest of all to believe.

Already the whole thing was beginning to seem unreal. We looked down at the fading panorama of Chile and compared it with the penciled dots on the map, but the places we had been were only names now: the Tolten, the Quesapu, the Maule. The smoking volcanoes, the pink flamingos flapping past the snowbanks, the great trout rushing out of water to a fly, were part of a dream. We had to be in Chile to make the dream come true.

Nineteen

Joyful for Angling

Of course this is a Corey Ford book. Of course this book's chock-full of his fishing stories; you bought it because, like you, Corey was a devout fisherman. Like you, he was an avid sportsman. Like you, he had a grand sense of humor. And maybe also like you, he served our country in the armed forces. So, of course you know this story's by Corey Ford. But you probably didn't know he was a major in the United States Army Air Corps during World War II, and a lieutenant colonel by the time that branch of the service was re-christened the United States Air Force.

Corey Ford was the USAAC's official chronicler. He was wild to get in the heat of battle, and he did, soon after the war broke out. Enlisting when he was an old man of thirty-nine, Corey traveled the globe until the fighting was over, from Greenland to the Aleutians, India to the Marianas, China to England, Alaska and points unknown. His wartime stories, published in magazines such as *Collier's* and *The Saturday Evening Post*, brought home the reality of what it was to be out there, fighting, frightened, a million miles from friends and family, nevertheless rising above it all to do the job. These stories, and later Corey's war-inspired books such as *The Last Time I Saw Them*, *War Below Zero,* and *Short Cut to Tokyo*, spun an unbreakable thread. For those at home, that thread was something solid to hold on to while their men and boys were God-knows-where. They fought for victory; many didn't live to celebrate it.

It's those yellowed, brittle, fifty-year-old papers of Corey's I read that moved me almost as much as his classic hunting story, "The Road to Tinkhamtown." Not just the stories. The letters—personal letters. Letters Corey wrote because he wanted to, felt a need to. He had to write to many folks and tell them their boy didn't make it. He'd say, "I knew your boy. He did you proud. He talked about you, all the time..." He probably felt they were helpless words, filled with empty comfort. I wonder if he ever knew how much they must have meant to a grief-stricken mother and father. These fliers and fighters and grease monkeys were just kids—eighteen, nineteen—like you, maybe, back then.

Corey risked his life to tell their stories, to offer a shoulder, to slap the guys on the back with encouragement when courage was a too-precious commodity. He remained, until the day he died, staunchly devoted to the Air Force. He said the most gratifying thing he ever did was to stand proudly in the shadow of those men and boys, each a hero, and any man who served in the USAF was simply one of the best fellows that ever lived. Corey put his money where his mouth was, too—he arranged that all royalties accrued from his wartime writings were to be paid directly into the Air Force Aid Society, a fund for the widows and children of fallen fliers.

Humor always triumphed, and Corey made good use of his. But here's a twist—a funny story about him by the late J. Bryan, III, a writer and longtime friend of Corey's, relating a near-death incident when Corey was flying in an Air Corps plane across the Atlantic in 1944:

On one flight from Gander to Prestwick, an engine caught fire when they were at "Jones Corner," exactly halfway across. The situation was dicey for a while; even so, Ford should have known better than to describe it to Sullivan in a letter. The only sympathy he drew was, "What better place for an engine to catch fire? You have the whole damn Atlantic to put it out with."

So when you read "Joyful for Angling," which Corey wrote while assigned to a B29 bomber crew during the Korean Conflict, delight in this fishing story, because it is delightful. Chuckle, because it's humorous. The story is pretty straightforward, about a bunch of fliers who take a break from risking every moment of every day of their lives in defense of our country.

It's a never-ending story; our boys are still out there, looking out for America, for our freedoms.

The loaded bomber had just picked up the formation and was departing on course for the target when Sgt. Sheets, the left scanner, called over the intercom that the number two engine was smoking. Capt. Art Hughes, the airplane commander, had noticed that the manifold pressure was beginning to drop, and about the same time, another B29 in the formation, flying on the left side of the box, reported that they could see flames coming out of Hughes' wing on the outboard side. The pressure was falling off fast, and Sgt. Edwards, the engineer, told Hughes that he should feather number two...

*A*rt Hughes flicked his rod, sent the enameld line forward through the guides and dropped a number ten Fanwing Coachman near a sunken log. The fly sank after a moment, and he retrieved it. From the adjoining skiff, Capt. Paul Hesler, the co-pilot, called to us, "There was a nice rise just beyond you, about ten o'clock."

"Right rudder," Art Hughes said to me, and I pulled hard on the right oar. "Now steer about ten degrees left." The boat nudged into the shadows along the shore. The sun was setting behind the peak of the volcano, and the wind had died down; the only sound was a party of Japanese fishermen, drunk on *saki*, sculling along the opposite shore of the lake and singing a wierd minor-key chant. The trout were breaking around the boat, and you tried to think of fishing; you tried not to think of flying over Korea two days ago in a crippled bomber and watching the smoke trailing from its wing and feeling the slight, ominous jar as the pilot lowered the nosewheel gear to clear an exit in case of a bailout...

"Ease off on the power," Art told me, and I rested the oars. He stood up in the stern, casting toward the widening circles where the trout had risen. "Just let the boat drift."

You tried to see the fly on the water, and you tried not to see the feathered props of the number two engine, standing rigidly at attention against the sky. The B29 had dropped out of formation because it was impossible to hold altitude with three engines and a full load of bombs. Edwards, the engineer, started depressurizing, everyone went on oxygen, and Art made for the coast because it is better to try to ditch at sea than to bail out over North Korea. The fire in the wing faded a little, and then blazed up again, and then, unaccountably, died out. After a couple of minutes, Art pulled up the nosewheel and headed back toward the target. Capt. McMacken, the bombardier, got off his load of five hundred-pounders accurately, and Lt. Black, the navigator, gave the heading home. So nothing happened, and it was just one of those routine incidents that takes place every day on a mission over Korea. Back in the States the next day, the papers carried the usual brief line: "Medium bombers again plastered enemy airfields around Pyongyang..."

"Mac's got one on," Art said suddenly, pointing to the other boat. McMacken's rod bent double as he brought the fish alongside, and Hesler, dropping the oars, reached out with a net and scooped a land-locked salmon out of the water. He held it aloft in the net, and we could see its silhouette for a moment against the darkening sky. Art called, "Nice going, Mac," and began casting again.

"Peaceful here," he said to me over his shoulder. "You'd never know there was a war."

The thing was to put the war out of your mind. Stop thinking about it. Forget the hardworking engines that might conk out on take-off or catch fire when you pushed them beyond their strength at 25,000 feet with ten tons of bombs. Forget the accurate enemy flak that blossomed ahead of you in black puffs, drawing nearer and nearer, radar-guided. Forget the enemy fighters that waited in MIG Alley, circling overhead at 40,000 feet, ready to scream down on the slow, vulnerable bombers. Forget the daily business of sweating the fog, and icing, and sudden violent thunder-storms that could shake the bombs loose in the bombbay, sweating the danger of mid-air collision with another airplane groping its way through the soup, sweating not making your rendezvous time with the fighter escort, sweating the weather over the target, sweating the dwindling gasload that must get you back to Japan. Forget the war. You're on rest leave now. For five days, here at Nikko Kanko, there's nothing to do but rest and relax...and fish.

Nikko Kanko is one of a number of former Japanese resort hotels that have been taken over as rest-and-recuperation centers for the armed forces in the Far East. The crew decided on Nikko Kanko when our pilot, an ardent angler and skilled hand with a fly rod, showed us a large colored poster he found advertising the resort: "Come to beautiful Nikko Kanko in the Japan Alps," it read. "Rainbow trout imported from the U.S.A." There was a lurid painting of a rainbow tinted a poisonous tomato red, seemingly suspended in space halfway down a waterfall. Under it, in the best Nipponese English, was the enthusiastic slogan: "Joyful for angling, nice for looking, good for tasting."

So we had come here, to beautiful Nikko Kanko, for the joyful angling, and for the first rest leave the crew had since they started flying combat. There is not much chance for rest when you are flying daily missions at an Air Force base. There are no Saturdays or Sundays off, and the men work day and night, around the clock, sleeping with the sound of airplane engines. After a while, their nerves get tight and they smoke too much and they get to flying airplanes in their sleep. A little relaxation is necessary medicine, even though it only lasts five days—five days can go very fast when you are heading back into combat as soon as they are over.

We had made a special trip to Tokyo in search of fishing tackle. Good gear is hard to locate in Japan; we had wandered up and down the Ginza for hours with a fistful of yen before we found a rod, at last, in the tackle store of Mr. Tosaku. It was coated with red lacquer and bound with exotic purple thread, but the action was not bad. We were lucky enough to purchase a stateside reel—the average Japanese reel is made of tin and sounds like a broken pencil sharpener—and by great good fortune, Mr. Tosaku had one skein of imported enameled line. It had no taper and was heavy enough to beach a tarpon, but it cast better than cotton thread. At the rear of the store was a huge bin of articificial flies, beautifully tied, that Mr. Tosaku scooped into a paper bag and sold by the pound like popcorn. We thought we had stumbled on an angler's dream until we discovered later that the hackle was soft as down, and the flies matted and sank as soon as they hit the water. Mr. Tosaku was reluctant to sell us a net. "You will not need a net," he smiled. "The rainbow at Nikko are too big for a net."

I wondered where I'd heard *that* one before.

Eight of us took off from the base the following morning; the other four members of the crew elected to go to a rest-hotel near Tokyo. It was a five-hour drive, counting the occasional stops for cold Japanese beer to overcome the dust and the smell of the overripe, honey-wagons trundling along the road in endless procession. The last half-hour was hairy indeed, with thirty-three hairpin turns so tight that we had to back the car up until the rear wheels dangled over space. "I'd rather drive this in an airplane," Ted Black said dubiously.

Nikko Kanko is at 5,000 feet and Lake Yunoko, where the fishing was best, was five miles beyond it—straight up. It was wild, spectacular country, full of bear and deer, dotted with small lakes and connecting streams that the Japanese government had joyfully stocked with rainbow trout, imported from the U.S., brook trout, and a small species of land-locked salmon that never seemed to get larger than twelve or fourteen inches. The rainbow, on the other hand, grew to prodigious size. When a Japanese takes a record fish, he smears its side with black ink and rolls it on a square of rice-paper. They showed us the imprints of several rainbow that could have gone eight or ten pounds. As a conservation measure, the stream itself was restricted to fly fishing only. The roadside sign warned the trespasser courteously: "Notice to Angler: No worm in the brook can be caught as fishing bait."

Art, a superb pilot, had the instinctive rhythm and sense of timing and depth-perception that go into fly casting, and in two hours he was putting his lure across the lake like a veteran. He balanced in the stern, in green squadron cap, flying coveralls, and heavy GI shoes, frowning at the shore.

"Give a little shove on the oars," he whispered to me. "A big one rose just ahead."

He dropped his fly accurately over the bubbles in the water. It floated for a moment, and then a sudden swirl sucked it down. Art lifted the tip of the rod and set the hook. The line began to cut across the surface of the lake and the reel screamed. Then, suddenly, the water exploded and the rainbow emerged, shaking its head to dislodge the barb, arched in a shower of drops, and dove again. Mac and Paul rowed nearer to watch the fight. Little by little Art worked it in, and I slipped the net under it and lifted it into the boat. Art sat down quite suddenly and lit a cigarette.

"Goddamn," he said. "I had to come all the way to Japan to catch my first trout."

We had the trout for breakfast the morning of the final day. The Japanese chefs cooked it to perfection with a sauce of butter and lemon and Worcestershire; it was good for tasting. We ate hurriedly; the car was waiting to take us back to the base. There would be a mission tomorrow.

Tomorrow there would be the usual briefing at three a.m., and then the crew would go out to the hardstand where the loaded bomber was waiting. After inspection they would climb into the airplane and take their places, Mac in the bombardier's seat in the nose, Paul on the right, Art on the left, with his long fingers working the controls, and Edwards at the engineer's panel. Ted Black would be behind him at the navigator's table, and the bomber would taxi down to the end of the strip and run its engines up. At o-six-hundred it would start lumbering down the tire-scarred runway, slowly gathering speed, straining to lift its load of bombs, taking off at last and heading westward over Japan—over the very moutains where we had been fishing. Over the Yellow Sea to Korea, and the flak-guns, and the waiting MIGS...

Art glanced at his watch. "Let's go, gang," he said. "Let's get airborne."

We picked up our B4 bags and carried them out to the car. The joyful angling was over.

I have seen better waters. I have caught bigger trout. But for five days, I had been with the finest crew I've ever known, and that was the best fishing trip I ever had.

Twenty

The Swedes Have a Way with Fish

You fish. You catch a fish, sometimes. Sometimes you catch and release; sometimes the fish releases when you want to catch. Yet seldom does a book about fishing got the extra mile to tell you what to do when you beat the odds and catch a fish. Well, look no further. Here are some cooking instructions about what to do with your fish now that you finally caught one.

Show this book to your wife, significant other, girlfriend, or companion. She'll be thrilled you finally bought a book that has something in it for her, too. Conversely, maybe you are a sportswoman who fishes, and your husband is a gourmet chef.

It's ironic that Corey wrote about cooking because he didn't know how to cook and always hired someone else to do the cooking. During the carefree days of his twenties, the Roaring Twenties, he'd wend his way up and down the streets of Manhattan seeking liquid refreshment at places such as the 21 Club and Moriarty's. Later, he spent considerable time downtown at the Players' Club, probably because of its distinguished membership, distinguished fare, and distinguished bar. He downed Scotch with Humphrey Bogart, Spencer Tracy, and Jimmy Cagney. Corey's "other" life was spent on the other coast—in Hollywood—where he wrote screenplays alongside a pal named Scott: F. Scott Fitzgerald, that is.

Anyway, it's nice to have a fishing book that shows the end to the means—how to cook what you catch. And it's nice to publish, finally, the only piece I know of by Corey Ford about cooking.

*A*ll my life I've been taking trout on a fly, and all my life (well, most of if) I've been removing the fly and turning the trout loose again. Fishing is for fun, I've always held, and not for food. Oh, I can go along with a lobster, or a shore-dinner now and then, but by and large, I'd prefer a good steak any time. Frankly, fish has never been my meat.

Which puts me in a class with most Americans who look at fish with about as much enthusiasm as bread pudding. People eat it because it is inexpensive or because it is supposed to be brainfodder, or because they are reducing, or because it's Friday—not because they enjoy it. Despite the fact that we have the greatest abundance and variety of seafood of any country in the world, our annual consumption averages only ten pounds per capita, less than any other country. Why this national indifference to aquatic fare, commercial fishermen wonder? How come we don't go for fish?

Tore Wretman, Sweden's foremost restauranteur, has an answer: "Most Americans do not know how good fish can taste," he suggested to me during luncheon at his famous Cafe Riche in Stockholm, "because they cook it so it does not taste like fish. Either they fry it until it is brittle, or boil it like a potato, or chop it up for chowder. In America, you try to disguise its flavor. Here in Sweden, we try to bring it out." He ran his eye casually over the day's menu. "Take Roding à la Riche, for example."

Roding is Sweden's native red char, first cousin to our own brook trout, the selfsame fish that I have been returning to the stream all these years. Through the wizardry of a Swedish chef, it had been transformed into as delectable a concoction as ever crossed my tonsils. There would be dancing in the streets of Gloucester, I reflected, if we could make fish taste like this back in the States. Would Mr. Wretman confide the secret?

"There is no secret," he shrugged. "The recipe is simplicity itself. Anyone can prepare it at home." He led me to the Riche's immaculate kitchen, bright with chrome and gleaming copper, where a white-capped impresario was in the process of cleaning a trout by wiping it with a towel dipped in oil. "Never soak a trout in water," Mr. Wretman warned me in an aside, "because it destroys the character." I watched the chef open it from the back, remove the spine and other main bones, and flatten it on its belly on a buttered silver platter approximately the size of the fish itself. Nothing difficult so far, I noted. Next he prepared a solid paste of butter, egg yolk, *mi de pain* (soft centers of bread), finely chopped shallots and parsley, salt and white pepper. "If shallots are difficult to obtain," Mr. Wretman explained, "scallions or small, mild white onions will do as well." The chef spread this mixture on the fish in an even layer, put some pats of butter on top, poured a dry white wine around it, and slid the platter into a hot oven. "Let it bake until the meat is cooked through and the surface nicely browned," Mr. Wretman concluded, "and then dust it with parsley and serve it on the same platter in which it was cooked." And that, fellow-fishermen, is all you need to know in order to parlay your next trout into a feast for the gods.

Granted, fish has always been a staple of the Swedish diet—so much so, in fact, that half a century ago the law specifically stated that servants and farmhands should not have to eat salmon more than four times a week. In the lovely old port city of Göteborg, noted for its export of seafood, the early-morning fish bazaar is conducted with all the pomp and circumstance of an art auction at a Park Avenue gallery. Sturdy fishing boats tie up alongside the pier at dawn, their winches creaking as they hoist cases of fresh fish out of the holds. Under the metal awning of the block-long warehouse are the multi-colored products of yesterday's catch, displayed side by side in neat rows on chunks of ice: turbot, a favorite delicacy in Scandinavia; red char from Vattern; salmon from north and east Sweden, Dover sole; plaice, whiting, which is taken during the spring months only; Baltic herring; mackerel, cod, and ling cod, the lutfisk that is Sweden's traditional Christmas Eve dish. There are tiny Danish shrimp that live in the seaweed of the North Sea, the size and sweetness of raspberries; live crabs, lobster, and crayfish. Hoses play constantly over the worn planking—the Swedes have a passion for cleanliness—and the sing-song voice of the auctioneer rises above the steady cacophony of thumping gasoline engines, tooting whistles, screaming seagulls, rattling handcarts wheeling away the cases of fish to waiting trucks that whisk them to retail markets and thence still fresh to the kitchen.

Granted, too, that Sweden's culinary art has come a long way since the old Viking method of eating fish, which was to hold it in both hands like an ear of corn and devour it while it is still flapping. Today there are no greater masters of cookery in the world than the Swedes—and, lest the French bristle, the Swedes themselves are the first to admit that the Gallic influence is predominant in most of their recipes. During the reign of Gustav III in the 18th century, the language of France was used by the upper classes, and Parisian cuisine was adopted by all the local chefs. Sauce Bernaise, it is claimed, was invented by the legendary chef, Pierre Bichard, to tickle the palate of Sweden's first Bernadotte. But in one area the Swedes have surpassed even their French tutors; when it comes to preparing fish, they are without peer. I'd long heard of Swedish cooking from Stateside gourmets and *feinschmeckers* who insisted that the seafood dishes of Sweden were, in a word, unbelievable. Well, I was skeptical, but I was willing to be convinced. Perhaps there were some tricks that I could learn. Not that I have any pretensions as a chef, let me hastily explain. I'm no frustrated Escoffier, yearning to indulge in mystic rites over a skillet. I don't even even like to cook, but I do like to enjoy what I eat. So I embarked on a sort of gastronomic tour of Sweden, visiting the palaces of gustatory pleasure and prevailing on the chefs to reveal their closely guarded recipes.

All the recipes quoted below are simple enough to be followed by an amateur cook, such as myself. All the fish I have selected are native to the United States except the sole, which does not occur on this side of the Atlantic, but halibut or flounder, which are usually sold as sole, can be substituted. The only ingredient that might be difficult to obtain is dill, the national herb of Sweden, and an essential element in most Swedish recipes. Dill is a tall, feathery plant resembling asparagus fern, and the Swedes discard the thick stalks and crowns of flowers and use only the tender leaves. Epicures hold it in such esteem that when Marlene Dietrich left Stockholm after a visit, her friends at the airport presented her, not with a bouquet of roses, but with an armload of newly cut dill. "A Swedish gourmet would no more think of serving salmon without dill," Tore Wretman stated flatly, "than of starting a meal without aquavit." Dill is so little known in our own country that most Americans think it is a pickle, but fresh dill (never use dried) is available in the markets of the larger cities, and it will grow anywhere that parsley grows. A ten-cent pack of dill seed, scattered in the garden, will give you a bountiful supply for the season.

A final word: If possible, avoid using frozen and packaged fish. Perhaps the real secret of Swedish cooking is the fact that their fish are freshly caught.

Sole (Sjotunga)

I've always had a theory that most great recipes are discovered by accident. Some years ago, for instance, I caught some walleyes in Ontario and gave them to the camp cook, the wife of my guide, to prepare for lunch. They arrived at the table exuding a delicious but indefinable aroma, and later I went into the kitchen to find out what wonderful new ingredient had been added. In considerable embarrassment, the cook confessed that, with typical French-Canadian thrift, she had fried them in some fat left over after baking a ham studded with cloves. Since then, I have always scattered a few cloves in the pan whenever I fry a fish.

By similar chance, I suppose, a Swedish chef may have stumbled on the recipe for the butter-filled fillet of lemon sole that was served aboard the Swedish American liner, Gripsholm. The Gripsholm is said to ride several inches lower in the water at the end of an Atlantic crossing due to the accumulated weight of its passengers who have partaken of the luxurious meals and midnight smorgasbords. But of all the varied dishes on the menu, the *filet de sole* had such a unique flavor that I sought out Chief Steward Stig Lundgren and asked what it was. "Curry," Mr. Lundgren replied, and obligingly divulged the magic formula. Preparing the sole itself is not complicated. Sprinkle each fillet with salt, dip a butter pat in chopped parsley, place it in the middle, and fold the fillet around it and flour it. Whip an egg, dip the fillet in it, roll in breadcrumbs to cover it completely, and fry in not-too hot shortening. What makes it so special is the sauce, prepared as follows (for eight fillets):

    4 egg yolks
    1 cup butter
    ½ teaspoon taragon vinegar
    1 teaspoon chopped taragon
    1 teaspoon bouillon extract
    1 teaspoon curry powder
    2 tablespoons water

Melt the butter and keep it hot. Place egg yolks, vinegar, water, and curry powder in a saucepan and beat steadily over low heat until the mixture is thick. Remove the pan from heat and add the melted butter slowly under medium temperature. Finally, add the bouillon and the taragon. Serve—and marvel.

Herring (Sill)

It as also aboard the Gripsholm that I became acquainted with the Swedish method of cooking herring in a buttered paper bag, called *Sill i pepper.* I suppose any glossy brown paper would do, if it is thoroughly greased. Here is Mr. Lundgren's recipe, equally easy to prepare:

Bone your salt herring and soak it in water overnight. Take two fillets of herring for each portion, lay them on a buttered paper, and between the pair of fillets place a slice of boiled potato and a slice of onion sauteed in butter. Fold the paper around the fish to form an airtight bag; pan-fry in shortening, and lift out carefully to preserve the aromatic steam until the bag is opened at the table.

Cod (Torsk)

What would constitute a Gentleman's Dinner in Sweden? I mean, which fish would a true gourmet choose above all others for his personal pleasure? The answer is cod—that same, lowly cod that we in the States grind up into fishcakes and fry in deep fat, a gastronomic bomb comparable only to that other American horror, fried clams. Not in Sweden, though. The connoisseur of fine foods, left to his own devices, would probably order some such menu as this:

Snaps (aquavit) and Stout (Porter);
Oysters with lemon slice;
More Snaps and Stout;
Fresh North Sea codfish, poached in thin slices and plenty of salt in
    the water, served with *skansk senapssas* (Scanian mustard sauce)
    and melted butter;
Mumma (Stout and Madeira, mixed);
Crepes Suzette;
Snaps;
Stout.

Mackerel (Makrill)

Say Sweden, and you think smorgasbord. This fine old Swedish custom is said to have started at country parties, where each arrival contributed his own homemade specialty to the community pile of food on a center table, around which the guests moved in an endless line, filling their plates over and over until they were no longer able to walk. Today, Sweden's chefs vie with one another to provide the most elaborate and varied smorgasbords; but the buffet at Henriksberg, the oldest and finest restaurant in Göteborg, included a particularly memorable item called Fish in Aspic *(Fisk i gele)*. The fish I had was mackerel, but salmon or, if you want to be exotic, eel, can be substituted. Although designed as an *hors d'oeuvre,* this could also serve as a novel hot-weather luncheon dish.

To prepare *Fisk i gele*, cut the mackerel into one-inch slices and cook in a fish stock seasoned in the following proportions. To a quart of liquid, add:

1 tablespoon white vinegar
¾ tablespoon salt
5 allspice
5 peppercorns
1 bay leaf
chopped dill

After cooking, drain the stock and place the fish on a platter to cool. Prepare the aspic by soaking 2 tablespoons of gelatin in a saucepan of cold water. Beat in 3 egg whites and a pint of strained fish stock. Bring slowly to a boil, stirring constantly, then cover and allow to stand for 15 minutes. Strain, adding salt and white pepper to taste. Place sections of hard-boiled eggs, small cooked shrimp, and quartered tomatoes in an attractive pattern in the bottom of a mold, pour some of the aspic over it slowly, and let it jell. Lay the slices of cold fish on top, arranged like the spokes of a wheel, pour the remaining aspic over them, and chill in the mold. Invert onto a plate, serve with mayonnaise, and decorate with clusters of dill.

Cold Salmon (Gravlax)

Gravlax, which literally means "buried salmon," orginated in northern Sweden where, in ancient times, salmon was preserved by sprinkling it with salt and sugar and pepper, digging a hole in the ground, placing the salmon on a bed of dill, and covering it with more dill and the earth itself. Thus treated, it would stay fresh for weeks or even months. "The modern method of of preparing *gravlax* is essentially the same," Tore told me. "The salmon should be very fresh and of the best quality, which in Sweden would mean the spring. Select a salmon weighing between twenty and thirty pounds, and use the middle part of one side. Remove all bones, but leave the skin on, and wipe with a fresh towel dipped in oil. Then rub into the flesh a mixture of two parts sugar, one part salt, a good amount of crushed whole white pepper, and plenty of finely chopped dill. Put a layer of dill leaves in a not-too-shallow dish, as near as possible to the dimensions of the fish, cover it with more dill, and place on top of it a plank of sufficient weight so that the salmon will lie under slight preassure. Leave in a cool place, and turn it once or twice during the pressure period."

The length of this period is a matter of heated argument among aficionados. "Some *gravlax* lovers prefer only five hours," Mr. Wretman conceded, "but such a short time will produce a salmon that, in my personal opinion, is too raw. I think that up to twenty hours is better. If left longer than that, the fish will tend to dry and become hard."

When ready to serve, the salmon can either be carved like ordinary smoked salmon, though in somewhat heavier slices, or cut straight down crosswise in portions about an inch thick. "The skin of each portion should be cut off, leaving a bit of the flesh," Mr. Wretman added, "and these strips of skin should be dipped in oil and fried skin-side down in a very hot pan, and served hot with the cold fish."

A true *gravlax* lover prefers to make his own sauce at the table, and here and there at the Riche you will see a solemn-faced epicure bent over a small bowl beside his plate, mixing condiments in the following proportions: 1 tablespoon of mild mustard (the very mildest available, Mr. Wretman insisted, and rather sweet), 1 tablespoon sugar, 1½ tablespoons wine vinegar, and a little pepper and salt. Into this mixture he pours about ⅛ pint of oil (not olive oil) while whipping it vigorously with a fork until it has the consistency of a light mayonnaise. At the last moment, he adds a few drops of lemon and, of course, some chopped dill. "Our national herb is absolutely necessary for the preparation of *gravlax*," Mr. Wretman pointed out sternly, "and nothing else can be substitiuted."

Hot Salmon (Lax najad)

On the northern outskirts of Stockholm, a half-hour's drive from the Riche, is an equally renowned restaurant, also owned by Tore Wretman, called the *Stallmastargarden* (stablemaster's yard). This is the oldest wooden structure in, or around, Stockholm, built in 1620 by the Lord High Admiral Gyllenhielm, half-brother of Sweden's famous King Gustav Adolf II as a home for his favorite stablemaster. It is a lovely, rambling manor house in Sweden's early seventeenth century architectural style, situated in a green oasis on the shore of Brunnsviken Bay and shaded by four linden trees planted by Gustav Adolf's daughter, regent Queen Christina. *Stallmastargarden* has been an inn for centuries, and its recipes are as traditional as the building itself. But the *specialité de la maison* is the smoked salmon, *lax najed,* which I consider, beyond a doubt, the finest fish dish I have ever tasted. With that native reticence that characterizes the Swedes, Mr. Wretman neglected to tell me that he himself invented the recipe, for which he has recieved numerous prizes. Through his generosity, it is published here for what I believe is the first time:

    1 middle part of one side of salmon about 2 pounds
    ½ pint white wine
    ½ pint fish broth
    parsley
    dill
    2 shallots
    1 pound leaf spinach
    ½ pint hollandaise sauce

The salmon should be very lightly salted, and then cured in cold smoke, preferably juniper, for 1½ hours so that it has only a very faint smoky taste. Place the salmon in an earthenware ovenproof dish, just big enough to hold the fish with the skin side turned up. Around the fish put the chopped shallots and a few branches of parsley, and add the white wine and fish broth. Cover with buttered paper and the lid of the dish, bring to a boil, and continue boiling until the fish is cooked through—— for a two-pound fish, this should be about fifteen minutes. When the salmon is ready, pour off the broth and reduce the liquid to half its volume by boiling. Thicken the broth with *buerre manie* to obtain a light sauce, and mix half of it with the hollandaise and chopped dill. Remove the skin from the salmon, place the fish on a layer of leaf spinich (parboiled then sauteed lightly in browned butter), and pour the other half of the sauce over it. Serve the mixed hollandaise on the side.

These, then, are some of the outstanding Swedish recipes that you could prepare as well in the States. All you need is a little luck—and lots of dill. And from now on you won't see me putting back many more trout. I've learned that eating fish can be fun, too.

Twenty-One

There'll Always Be a Scarface

There are a few lines in literature that are remarkable, even when isolated from the context in which they appear—lines that have the power to jerk a heartstring and cause the soul to swell or a tear to come to the eye. "Call me Ishmail" and, "I alone am here to tell thee." "I am born." "Follow me and I will make you fishers of men." "You're a better man than I am, Gunga Din," and, "Come live with me and be my love..."

I've added the last line of this story to my personal list. It strikes the same kind of chord—something to do with humility, hope, goodness, courage, grace, and love.

Think about *why* you fish.

It's the humble beauty found in nature, and the hope of grabbing—if only for an afternoon—a little peace. It's the goodness found in the companionship of your best fishing buddy. It's the courage to stand the test of time as you wait, often in vain, to hook the big one. It's grace—that word no one seems to know how to define—that has something to do with the simple enjoyment of living. And loving life. Yes, life can be pretty good to a fisherman.

Man built no cathedral or temple equal to the majesty of a copse of mighty, soaring pines. See if you don't agree next time you're under a regal conifer about to cast a line into sparkling waters. Watch how the sun filters through the boughs. Kind of like the glow that reflects off the panes of stained-glass windows, kind of holy. Fishing's nothing less than a religion—and that makes you, my friend, a member of the faith—baptized in the waters of a trout stream.

Thoreau said, "Time is but the stream I go a-fishing in."

Here's to you then, dear Angler, and time, and plenty of it, to go a-fishing—all the rest of your life.

$\mathcal{I}$t isn't the ones you keep. It's the ones that get away—the trophy shots you miss, the record trout that slip out of the net—that you remember all your life.

I've killed my share of big gobblers, but the turkey I recall most vividly was an old granddaddy who sailed past my gun into the Carolina sunset, his beard dangling a foot below his chest. I've taken my toll of rainbow trout, but I can still see a certain pink-sided monster dancing away across Stewart Lake at the end of a broken line, jangling the metal spoon still hooked in his jaw. There was the huge Kenai moose that almost, but not quite, came within range of my rifle. There was the salmon I lost once on the Miramichi.

And there'll always be Old Scarface in a weed cover of Lake of the Woods.

I can say without hesitation that Scarface is the largest muskie in Ontario, because there is nobody—at least, at this writing—able to dispute me. Forty pounds, fifty, sixty; make it what you will. The scar on his right cheek, from which he got his name, is supposed to have been made when he struck savagely at a whirling propeller; I believe it was nothing less than the screw of an ocean liner, judging by the width of those gargantuan jaws. His mottled green side looked as big as a rowboat turning over. His squared tail was like the fluke of an anchor as he sounded.

It was Happy who led me to the cove where Scarface lay. Happy had been guiding in this Lake of the Woods country longer than he or anyone else can remember; he knows every channel and inlet of Ontario's famous fishing waters, and he knows off which rocky point the biggest muskies lie. What's more, he guards each hiding place as jealously as a prospector protecting a secret goldstrike. The muskie is a big-game animal, and like a lordly bull moose or a boss brown bear, he has his own range where he may live for years, driving off every rival male who invades his personal domain. For at least five years, Scarface had reigned supreme on the same weed-grown reef, Happy said. The high-priced plugs and spinners and feathered lures that decorated the bottom were a tribute to his uncanny acumen. None of Happy's customers had hooked him yet.

There was a trace of a smile on Happy's face as he mentioned this fact. I suspected that Happy had acquired a grudging admiration for the

the champ. Old guides get that way sometimes about a big muskie, Happy admitted, as he steered the boat through the swift bottleneck of Ash Rapids to the adjoining lake. Like Old Mose, for instance. Old Mose was a very young muskie when he showed up one fall at Jensen's fish camp across the lake. Jensen fed him all that winter with fish from his sucker box, and Mose grew quite tame and refused to leave. He lived in front of Jensen's pier for seventeen years, growing to record size, and Jensen used to stand on the dock with a shotgun and drive off any intruder who tried to catch him. Three times, Old Mose was hooked by poachers who sneaked in at night, but each time he broke loose and got away. The end came one summer when Mose grabbed a big bucktail streamer that pinned his upper and lower lips together so he couldn't eat. He drifted helplessly for days off the end of the pier, growing thinner and thinner, gazing up at Jensen with big sad eyes. At last he disappeared, and Jensen became so despondent that he sold his fish camp and married a girl in Kenora.

Our boat threaded the rapids, and we headed across open water to an island on the far side of the lake. Some fifty yards offshore, a submerged reef ran parallel to the island; a lone pink boulder on the beach marked its northern extremity. The water on the reef was so shallow that the tips of the green muskie cabbage showed above the surface, and waving green fronds drifted with the waves. Happy cut the motor and we glided slowly down the reef, casting right and left across the tangled weeds.

The surface of the water began to boil erratically just ahead of the boat, and a small school of walleyes splashed and leapt terror-stricken into the air. And then we saw it. The whole reef seemed to rise before us, a monstrous pair of jaws came out of the water to crunch one of the walleyes, a great greenish form curved in a following arc, and submerged again. The lake subsided. I looked at Happy. He looked at me. We let out our breath very slowly.

"Scarface," Happy said with a contented sigh.

I hammered the water the rest of the afternoon. I cast till my arms ached. I contributed my share of expensive hardware to the weedy bottom. We headed home at last when a rising wind churned the lake into whitecaps and drops of rain began to sting our cheeks. I huddled in the boat in wet silence as Happy ran the rapids and raced back to camp in the driving storm.

That night we built a fire in the cabin as rain pelted against the windows and the gale howled outside. I sat crosslegged on the cot, my left arm rammed inside an inverted leather combat boot, working the waterproofing dubbing into the seams. Happy stood in the doorway in a glistening sou'wester, gnawing a pipe stem.

"How big do you think Scarface would go, Happy?" I asked.

"Maybe six feet. Them big muskies never get much over that. The difference is in their girth. Scarface is fat, he'd be better'n fifty, sixty pounds."

"We'll get him tomorrow," I replied.

"Hope so," Harry sighed. "Wind's shifted into the east. Looks like a storm..."

The storm continued unabated all the rest of that week. The wind lashed the lake into a heaving sea, and great breakers rolled and crashed against the rocky shore. I tried casting from the ledge near the cabin, but the gusts whipped the plug back into my face. Once, during a lull, I moseyed down the shore to a protected cove and cast for walleyes; Happy cooked them over an open fire according to his own recipe, dipping the fillets in egg batter and sprinkling them with ground cloves. I have never tasted anything better. Day after day we waited for the gale to let up so we could return to the weedy reef where Scarface lay.

The sun broke through about noon of the last day. We sheared a propeller going through As Rapids; by the time we rowed back to camp and substituted a new one, the afternoon was almost gone. We thudded at full speed through the narrow stem of the hourglass and crossed the lake to the island. Abreast of the pink boulder, Happy chopped the motor and we drifted over the shoal reef, casting ahead.

A "V" of water shot toward my lure and suddenly my line was tight. I saw a green shoulder turn and the reel screamed as the heavy fish ran out his line, making for the top of the island. I braced my feet against the gunwales, my rod dipping dangerously, and checked the savage rush in the nick of time. The muskie turned and made for the boat, and I reeled in hastily.

The taut line hummed as it sliced the water in a circle around the bow. Little by little, its rushes grew more feeble, the green shape wallowed in the water, and I had a glimpse of a greenish-white belly against the submerged weeds. I brought the fish alongside, Happy poised his blunt wooden persuader in mid-air and struck the back of its skull with a solid thump. He grabbed it behind the gills and hauled the limp muskie over the side.

We gazed at it, a little disappointed. It was a good muskie, but no giant; perhaps forty inches in length, not more than thirty pounds. From all the legend that had built up around Old Scarface, we had taken for granted that it would be a record fish. We rolled it over, but there was no sign of a scar on its smooth white cheeks. Even that colorful legend was false. It just went to show what liars fishermen are.

"Maybe we could stuff a jackfish down its throat to make it weigh more," Happy winked as he spun the outboard motor to start it. "That's how a lot of dudes work it. I was weighing a big muskie last year, and thirty-six spark plugs fell out of its stomach."

He swung the boat around and headed back across the reef toward the lake. The sun was down, and a last orange-yellow twilight touched the surface of the water with gold. We turned and looked back regretfully at the pink boulder and the silent weeds offshore. And then, suddenly, the weeds were sucked down in a mighty swirl, the waters parted—and Old Scarface rose. He seemed to hang suspended in the air, silhouetted against the sunset, as permanent as a mounted fish over a mantel. Then he dove again with a final insolent flick of his anchor-wide tail.

That is the fish I'll see all the rest of my life.

Afterword

I first met Corey Ford, like a lot of you, in the pages of *Field & Stream*, in his "Minutes of the Lower Forty" monthly column. I was a tad too young to appreciate his other works, especially his humor and parody and his thirty books; by the time I was old enough to find delight in them, he was already gone.

I met Corey Ford again years later, when I was involved in the re-release of a collection of his works called *The Corey Ford Sporting Treasury*. I got to know Dr. James W. Hall, III, the original "Doc Hall" character from "The Lower Forty," and to appreciate Corey as not only the consummate outdoorsman, but also one of the finest writers of his and any other time.

Outside of my on-going friendship with Doc, Corey faded for me, until Doc called me at home one night with the news that he had been contacted by a woman in Freedom, New Hampshire, the sleepy little New England town that Corey had adopted and renamed Hardscrabble and used as the backdrop for his "Lower Forty" stories. Turns out, that woman, Laurie Morrow, and her family own the forty-acre patch of low ground that Corey called the Lower Forty; the house Corey once owned is next door.

All very nice, I thought. But then came the surprise—Laurie had been given the exclusive right to be Corey's biographer by Dartmouth College, the heir to Corey's literary estate, and had been rummaging through the boxes of files at the Dartmouth Library. There she had discovered hundreds of unpublished manuscripts by the great man, enough for a number of books.

I was on a plane to New Hampshire almost immediately.

Some of the stories Laurie unearthed have been published in magazines—with a life of one month—others have never been published at all. There were even four versions of his famous and touching "Road to

Tinkhamtown," which many regard as the finest sporting short story ever written. That story will be told in a book yet to come.

Corey's wishes were for any material he had willed to the college to be published or republished, with the proceeds to be earmarked for some special charitable projects at Dartmouth. This book is the first of such endeavors.

Corey Ford lived in a gentler time, a time of split-cane rods and sweet-breathed setters and Parker shotguns. Late in his life, he was something of a country squire. He'd made his money, and lived out his days fishing and wingshooting around the globe. He looked at everything with a cocked eye, slightly off-center from the way the rest of the world viewed things, and his fishing adventures were no different.

With pal Alastair McBain, the foil for many of the stories in this volume, he tried fishing in places that, in those times, were at the edge of the world—Alaska and Chile, for example. But he loved best the quiet waters near home.

Today's trout fishermen know nothing of drying and greasing lines, of silk leaders and tippets, and of cane rods that had their own beauty but little of the versatility of today's graphite and boron pieces. To be a fly fisherman in those days was an act of faith, for the work involved was prodigious compared with today's high-tech simplicity. Perhaps this was part of the lure for him. His tribe was small, those who fished with the fly, and I imagine he would have a few things to say and write about the chartreuse and hot-pink-clad "fishers" we see today, choking the Battenkill, the Madison, and the Au Sable.

But these folks—I among them—who commit the great act of fly fishing owe a debt to those who came before us, who developed the craft to a form, like a fine London shotgun, that has not changed in decades, because it was made perfect so many years ago.

I hope you've enjoyed this book. Others will follow, including a wingshooting book called *The Trickiest Thing in Feathers* to be released soon. After having read this book and those that follow, you will know something of the man and the era in which he lived.

Steve Smith
Traverse City, Michigam

Corey Ford Archives, courtesy of Dartmouth College .